EOIN O'SULLIVAN

REIMAGINING
HOMELESSNESS

For Policy and Practice

POLICY PRESS SHORTS POLICY & PRACTICE

First published in Great Britain in 2020 by

Policy Press
University of Bristol
1–9 Old Park Hill
Bristol
BS2 8BB
UK
t: +44 (0)117 954 5940
pp-info@bristol.ac.uk
www.policypress.co.uk

North America office:
Policy Press
c/o The University of Chicago Press
1427 East 60th Street
Chicago, IL 60637, USA
t: +1 773 702 7700
f: +1 773-702-9756
sales@press.uchicago.edu
www.press.uchicago.edu

British Library Cataloguing in Publication Data
A catalogue record for this book is available from the British Library

Library of Congress Cataloging-in-Publication Data
A catalog record for this book has been requested

ISBN 978-1-4473-5351-5 paperback
ISBN 978-1-4473-5352-2 ePub
ISBN 978-1-4473-5354-6 ePdf

Cover design by Policy Press
Front cover image: iStock
Printed and bound in Great Britain by CMP, Poole
Policy Press uses environmentally responsible print partners.

Contents

Acknowledgements

I would like to thank: Policy Press for their forbearance; Mike Allen, Volker Busch-Geertsema, Catherine Conlon, Sarah Craig, Ian O'Donnell and Cameron Parsell for reading and commenting on various draft chapters; members of the European Observatory on Homelessness for their insights over the past 25 years; Guy Johnson for his conviviality, conversations and coffee in Melbourne; Dennis Culhane for his generosity, good company and sharing with me in many locations over many years his knowledge of homelessness; and Courtney Marsh for her editorial assistance.

ONE

Recollecting homelessness

Introduction

I first started thinking about homelessness in the late 1980s when I started working in a 15-bed male night shelter, Fairgreen House, in Galway, a medium-sized city in the West of Ireland. I was in my second year at the local university studying sociology, politics and history, and I got involved following a suggestion from a school friend. I had no idea at the time that my experience in the shelter would shape my research on homelessness, coercive institutions and the management of marginality for the next 30 years.

The shelter was jointly managed by two voluntary, or not-for-profit, bodies – the Galway Social Services Council (now known as COPE) and the Galway Simon Community – and had opened in June 1983, replacing an earlier temporary shelter on the same site. In my eyes, the shelter population was largely, in Bahr and Caplow's (1973) evocative description, a relatively small group of 'old men drunk and sober', but from my initial working experience, particularly on a Wednesday evening after receiving their weekly social welfare payment, they were more likely to be drunk than sober; if there was the consumption of drugs other than alcohol in the shelter, I was not aware of it.

When I later conducted a statistical analysis of the users of the shelter between 1983 and 1989, I learned to my surprise that over 1,000 different individuals, ranging in age from ten to 90, had stayed there for varying periods of time (O'Sullivan, 1993), and that more than half had one, usually very short, spell in the shelter and never returned. However, a very small number, less than 1 per cent, were virtually full-time residents, except when they spent short, but frequent, sojourns in prison, various psychiatric facilities and other institutional sites. This was an important finding but I did not appreciate its full significance until I later discovered the work of Dennis Culhane and colleagues on the patterns of shelter use (Culhane and Kuhn, 1998; Kuhn and Culhane, 1998).

This work, now replicated in a number of other cities (see Chapter Two), demonstrates conclusively that the majority of people who experience homelessness and need to utilise emergency accommodation do so for relatively short periods of time, and for once-off experiences. This is why the need to avoid equating the experience and profile of a small number of long-term shelter users with 'homelessness' is so important for researchers, front-line staff and policymakers alike as it distorts both our understanding of the nature of homelessness and how we respond, both individually and at a policy level. This is a core theme of this book. However, it is understandable why this occurs. Although it is 30 years since I worked in the shelter in Galway, I can recall with great clarity the long-term users of the shelter – all but one of whom, to the best of my knowledge, are now deceased – but I have limited or no recollection of the other hundreds of men that passed through the shelter during the time I worked there. The one long-term resident who is still alive – and from my naive perspective, the most chronic and entrenched shelter user, when he was not in prison for frequently breaking the window of a well-known local off-licence, among other minor offences – subsequently moved out of the shelter and now resides in his own permanent stable accommodation in Galway.

A small number of men slept rough in the city, mostly on a transitory basis when they were temporarily barred from the shelter, usually for acts of violence against fellow residents or staff. Some were barred on a long-term basis due to staff concerns about their propensity for violence, as well as, in hindsight, the inability of the small number of staff members to manage their often challenging behaviour in the confines of a shelter that was rudimentary in terms of facilities, and could be claustrophobic and chaotic. From memory, the staffing comprised four full-time extraordinarily committed and memorable individuals employed by the Galway Social Services Council, supplemented by what were termed 'full-time workers' from the Simon Community, who were equally memorable, and a floating number of well-intentioned volunteers colloquially known as co-workers (I was one of them but later went on to work in the shelter on a full-time paid basis for approximately a year).

Women experiencing homelessness barely featured in my world in Galway. A hostel with two rooms for women, Bethlehem House, was provided by the Legion of Mary, a voluntary Catholic organisation, but it only opened in the evening and the women had to vacate the premises early in the morning. There were also two facilities for women escaping gender-based violence but they seemed to me to be separate to homelessness services. Some of the women who stayed in the Legion of Mary hostel had partners or husbands in the male shelter that I worked in but my recollection is that the numbers were small. The fact that Sr Stanislaus Kennedy had published a pioneering account of women experiencing homelessness in Dublin in the mid-1980s (Kennedy, 1985) should have sensitised me to the different patterns of homelessness experienced by women, and that there were many 'unaccompanied' women experiencing homelessness, but my world at the time was the world of homeless men.

The number of unaccompanied young people experiencing homelessness was significant, both nationally and in Galway

(McCarthy and Conlon, 1988; O'Sullivan and Mayock, 2008), and a number of residential facilities operated in the town to provide care and accommodation for them (O'Kennedy, 2016). Legally, health and social care services had responsibility for young people up to 16 years of age, and housing authorities had responsibility for those aged 18 and over, so it was the 16 and 17 year olds who were particularly vulnerable to experiencing homelessness.

Families with accompanying child dependants experiencing homelessness were rare in Galway at this time, or so it seemed, and there were no emergency accommodation services for families; if they experienced homelessness, they were split up, with children accompanying the mother or being placed in care. This was also the case in the rest of the country; however, in 1990, for the first time, or certainly the first recorded instance, five families were placed in bed-and-breakfast (B&B) accommodation in the Greater Dublin region at a cost of £520, or nearly €1,150 at 2019 rates (Moore, 1994).

The situation in Galway, where virtually all residential services for those experiencing homelessness, both young people and adults, were provided by a variety of voluntary or not-for-profit bodies, was mirrored throughout the rest of the country (for an overview of services in Galway in the late 1980s, see Farrell, 1988). A small number of County Homes managed by local authorities – essentially workhouses that were renamed following political independence in the early 1920s – were also in operation, providing beds for men in buildings usually adjacent to the main Home, referred to as casual wards (Doherty, 1982). Indeed, St. Brendan's, the County Home in Loughrea in rural County Galway some 40 km from Galway City, was a regular port of call for the users of the shelter and an integral part of the 'institutional circuit' (Hopper, 1997) that a number of the shelter users navigated. In some of the casual wards, the men were locked in at night. One episodic user of Fairgreen House died in a casual ward in June 1988; the residents had been unable to summon assistance when he became ill as they were locked in with no means of contacting staff.

The majority of the users of the shelter, particularly the long-term users, had worked in England, almost exclusively as manual labourers, for significant periods of time (McCarthy, 1988). Many had also spent time in the various residential child welfare institutions, particularly Industrial Schools, that provided accommodation for nearly 6,000 children at any point in time during the first four decades after independence, and subsequently in the broader range of coercive institutions for adults, particularly prisons and psychiatric hospitals, which confined a minimum of 1 per cent of the Irish population in the mid-1950s (O'Sullivan and O'Donnell, 2012). Indeed, a number of shelter users had spent parts of their childhood in St. Joseph's Industrial School in nearby Salthill, which closed in 1995 after operating for 125 years.

The numbers 'coercively confined' (O'Sullivan and O'Donnell, 2007) progressively declined in these various institutions in the second half of the 20th century, and with the exception of the prison, they were in terminal decline by the time I took up work at Fairgreen House. In part, the shelter users with whom I was most familiar could be considered part of a cohort that experienced large-scale emigration in the 1950s and 1960s, as well as large-scale institutionalisation during the same period. With the demise and closure of the majority of institutions of confinement, a decline in demand for shelters for those experiencing homelessness could be expected; however, as detailed later in the book, while shelter use declined for this cohort, new groups emerged to take its place (See Culhane et al, 2013 for an account of a similar process in the United States).

During the period in which I worked at the shelter, it appeared (to me at any rate) that an increasing number of shelter users were coming from the large psychiatric hospital in the east of the county, St. Brigid's, which was in the process of decanting its residents as part a national programme of deinstitutionalisation (Walsh, 2015); indeed, the deinstitutionalisation of such patients is often cited as an explanation for increased rates of homelessness in the 1980s and 1990s in Ireland and elsewhere in the Global North. However, on closer examination, St. Brigid's, which had an in-patient population of over 1,600 in the late 1950s, had steadily reduced its patient numbers over a prolonged period of time. By the time I was working at the shelter, the in-patient population of St. Brigid's had reduced to 400, and it eventually closed in 2013 after 180 years in operation.

In hindsight, this should have alerted me to the importance of a temporal understanding of the dynamics of homelessness: if the systematic discharge of patients over 30 years had not resulted in surges of homelessness in the past, what was it about the period that I worked at the shelter that had resulted in an apparent increase in former patients ending up in emergency accommodation? It may have been that there was no upsurge, but rather that the immediacy of managing often disturbed individuals in the shelter distorted my perception, and that former patients of St. Brigid's were simply more troublesome than more numerous.

During my time working at the Fairgreen shelter, the legislative framework that determined the responsibility and response of the state for those experiencing homelessness was under review. Responsibility for young people experiencing homelessness was provided via the Children Act 1908, and for adults, limited statutory responsibility was provided under the Health Act 1953 and the Housing Act 1966; however, in practice, the division of responsibility between the health and housing authorities resulted in neither authority responding adequately to those experiencing homelessness (Harvey, 1985).

In 1988, a new Housing Act provided a broad definition of homelessness – persons who, in the opinion of the local authority, had no accommodation that they could reasonably occupy or were living in a night shelter or other such institution – and set out the responsibility of local authorities in respect of adults experiencing homelessness (Maher, 1989). The Housing Act 1988 also provided a stream of central government funding for those providing services to those experiencing homelessness, and in the first five years after the passing of the legislation, nearly £3 million was allocated through local authorities to the providers of services. Although rarely enforced by the Gardai (Police), homelessness, or 'wandering abroad' in the parlance of the Vagrancy (Ireland) Act 1847, was an offence, and the Housing Act 1988 decriminalised homelessness by deleting the relevant section of the Vagrancy Act 1847.

Although the Housing Act 1988 was designed to facilitate access to social housing for single persons experiencing homelessness, the construction of social housing plummeted in the period immediately after the passing of the legislation (Fitzgerald, 1990). This decline in the supply of social housing, the limited number of housing units for single people and competition from other vulnerable households for an increasingly scarce resource resulted in few single persons experiencing homelessness being allocated social housing tenancies. Instead, the largely unregulated and insecure private rented sector (O'Brien and Dillon, 1982), with the aid of a rent supplement from the Department of Social Welfare, was the primary means of exiting congregate shelter accommodation.

In brief, my vicarious experience of homelessness in the west of Ireland in the late 1980s and early 1990s chimed with broader patterns in the rest of the Global North. Those visibly experiencing homelessness were largely single males with a range of dysfunctions: some had been discharged from psychiatric hospitals following a process of deinstitutionalisation commencing in the late 1960s; others were literally homeless on the streets or episodically used congregate shelters and various other institutions – the primary response to meeting their needs was the provision of rudimentary congregate shelter facilities (for an overview of shelter services in the early 1980s, see O'Brien, 1981). Single women experiencing homelessness were encountered relatively rarely, largely as they were provided for in a parallel range of congregate residential facilities (O'Sullivan, 2016a) but not deemed part of the homelessness 'problem'. Families did experience homelessness but were significantly more likely to be allocated social housing tenancies than singles; those that were not, were likely to be split up and their children placed in care. Providers were primarily not-for-profit bodies and in as much as there was a discernible model or ideology underpinning these services, it was an attempt to promote sobriety and prepare for re-entry to 'mainstream society'.

After the Housing Act 1988

Over the quarter of a century or so after the passing of the Housing Act 1988, there was relatively little change in terms of service provision for adults experiencing homelessness in Ireland, and national data on the extent and composition of those experiencing homelessness were scant and inadequate. More robust data were available for Dublin; from the available sources, they were largely single men and their numbers were relatively low and stable (Fahey and Watson, 1995; Homeless Agency, 2006). Exchequer revenue funding for services for people experiencing homelessness increased steadily, rising from €3 million in 1995 to €55 million in 2010, and new dedicated funding streams for approved housing bodies (AHBs) to provide accommodation for those experiencing homelessness allowed for the construction of new purpose-built residential facilities, and the upgrading of existing residential services. For example, the shelter that I had worked at in Galway was demolished and replaced on roughly the same site in 2007 with a 26-bed facility with single rooms, rather than cubicles, and enhanced communal facilities, and is still operating today.

Casual wards ceased over this period, and with the exception of one shelter in Dublin managed by Dublin City Council, virtually all services for people experiencing homelessness, particularly residential services, were provided by not-for-profit bodies, the vast majority of which were funded, at least in part, by the central and local government. Despite the upgrading of facilities, the model of service provision remained much the same, with the majority of services content to manage single persons experiencing homelessness through the provision of large-scale congregate facilities in which stays were intended to be temporary; however, in many cases, this turned into long-term accommodation in the absence of viable alternatives (Kelleher et al, 1992). Others experiencing homelessness simply oscillated between various coercive institutions, the private rented sector and shelters. For the small, but steadily increasing, number of families, usually female-headed lone-parent families, the use of private providers, usually in the form of B&B-type accommodation, became more common but was still a relatively small part of the overall picture.

In terms of understanding homelessness, structural factors, such as housing and welfare policy, were beginning to be seen as increasingly important in understanding the pathways into homelessness and the barriers to exiting; however, this thinking was largely the preserve of a small number of advocacy groups such as Focus Point (now Focus Ireland) and others, many now defunct, such as the National Campaign for the Homeless and the Streetwise National Coalition. For the majority of con-gregate shelter providers, homelessness was largely a problem of 'inadequate' individuals with a range of disabilities who lacked family support, and the role of the shelter was to pro-vide a rudimentary roof over their head. From my experience of the shelter in Galway, 'treatment' was usually confined to referring individuals to psychiatric residential facilities or other detoxification residential centres to 'dry out', as well as encour-agement to attend Alcoholics Anonymous meetings following the period of 'drying out'.

For unaccompanied young people under 18 experiencing homelessness, the situation was to change radically. Following the gradual implementation of the Child Care Act 1991, which fundamentally reformed the child welfare system and made specific provision for young people experiencing homelessness (O'Sullivan, 1995), the number of young people, that is, those under 18, experiencing literal homelessness became exceedingly rare as a result of providing a range of suitable (and some not so suitable) accommodation and effective prevention. During this period, the last remnants of the large-scale system of residential provision for children were dismantled and foster care become the norm for children and young people needing out-of-home care. The fact that youth homelessness could be successfully reduced and large-scale residential institutions closed acted as a stimulus for policies in relation to adults experiencing homelessness.

During this period, I was now working in Dublin with a number of advocacy groups, and one of the initiatives was to pursue a series of High Court cases involving young people under the age of 18 in order to seek that their entitlement to accommodation under the provisions of Part 5 of the Child Care Act 1991 was vindicated. Ultimately, the High Court ruled that the individuals concerned needed secure accommodation as the health services claimed that no open residential facility could meet their needs, and a number of secure facilities were later opened – not the intended outcome! This experience of using the courts to direct social policy, and the unintended consequences of such tactics, would result in scepticism on my part of various attempts to direct policymakers via legal remedies, and the importance of instead generating a consensus to resolve such issues.

Ireland in comparative perspective

In the early 1990s, through participation in the European Observatory on Homelessness (EOH), a network of researchers across Europe, I broadened my understanding of homelessness. The profile of those experiencing homelessness varied significantly across the European Union (EU), and the varieties

Although the rate of the construction and acquisition of social housing gradually increased from 2015, demand substantially exceeded supply. As a consequence, demand for social housing was increasingly met via social housing supports, that is, various rent supplements to facilitate access to the private rented sector, rather than social housing tenancies. As discussed in more detail in Chapter Four, such social housing supports are inherently less secure than social housing tenancies as landlords in the private rented sector can legally terminate a tenancy with relative ease.

Equally, the full gamut of standard responses were deployed, including additional emergency accommodation, preventative services and an extraordinary range of street-level responses, particularly in Dublin where the issue is most acute. Dedicated central and local government expenditure on preventative services, emergency accommodation and other services designed to assist households exit homelessness has increased by over 200 per cent, from just under €70 million in 2013 to just over €216 million in 2019, and this figure excludes both revenue generated by various NGOs through fundraising and other exchequer-funded general social housing schemes that households experiencing homelessness can avail themselves of.

The number and composition of households experiencing homelessness in Ireland in 2020 is dramatically different to when I started working at Fairgreen House over 30 years ago. Some of the responses and providers remain the same, but they have been supplemented with new services and new providers. No longer the preserve of largely single, middle-aged men – at least in its public manifestation, with women experiencing more 'hidden' forms of homelessness – female-headed households now make up an ever-increasing share of those experiencing homelessness in shelters and other emergency and temporary accommodation. Those experiencing homelessness are increasingly female, in their 20s and 30s, and have few, if any, disabilities or dysfunctions, with housing affordability being the key driver.

Emergency accommodation services are still provided by non-state actors but joining the not-for-profit sector are a growing number of private sector providers, providing emergency accommodation, primarily for families, in hotels and B&Bs at a cost of €2 million a week in the first half of 2019. As noted earlier, in 1990, five families were placed in this form of accommodation in Dublin; by mid-2019, four families *a day* were being placed in emergency accommodation in Dublin, the majority in B&B-type accommodation. Nationally, there were slightly more adults in B&B-type accommodation than in congregate shelters. Central government expenditure on services for people experiencing homelessness was less than €3 million in the five years between 1989 and 1993; in the first half of 2019, it was nearly €3 million a week, as detailed in Chapter Four. In addition to the ongoing provision of congregate shelters for singles, not-for-profit and for-profit providers are also delivering congregate accommodation for families in what are termed 'Family Hubs'.

Conclusion

The pace of change in Ireland over the past five years is comparatively unusual but reflects what has been happening in other jurisdictions over a longer time frame. That such change has occurred in such a concentrated period of time provides a timely opportunity to reflect on how we think about and respond to homelessness. Based on popular and media portrayals, we *imagine* that homelessness is the consequence of individual failings and dysfunctions. Responses to these rising numbers are variable across countries but broadly include elements of congregate emergency accommodation, long-term supported accommodation, street-based services such as the provision of soup and blankets, and degrees of coercion. Attempts to prevent homelessness from occurring in the first instance have gained prominence in some policy responses in other jurisdictions. There are some examples where homelessness has decreased, such as in Finland and Norway or in relation to veterans' homelessness in the US, but these are the exceptions rather than the rule (for further details, see Allen et al, 2020). In a recent overview, 24 of the 28 member states of the EU have reported an increase in the number of people experiencing homelessness over the past decade, with three reporting a mixed pattern or stabilisation, and only Finland experiencing a significant decrease (Baptista and Marlier, 2019: 45–9).

The core theme of this book is that policymakers, civil society organisations and the media need to *rethink* how we conceptualise and respond to homelessness. The number of people experiencing homelessness is rising in the majority of countries of the Global North. Using Ireland as a case study but situating the Irish experience in a comparative context, this book provides an accessible account of the contemporary drivers and demographics of homelessness, in particular: the feminisation of homelessness; the range of possible policy responses availed of and, equally importantly, not availed of; the impact of research evidence and data on policy and practice responses; the role of social media and new civil society organisations in constructing contradictory public images of homelessness; and why, despite increased policy prominence and provision, the number of households experiencing homelessness continues to rise. The belief that homelessness can be ended is increasingly gaining prominence 'through a reimagined approach that combines evidence, resources, innovative thinking, and political will' (Henwood et al, 2015: 3).

Drawing on contemporary research, policy and practice, this book aims to impact on how policymakers and practitioners think about and respond to homelessness, with the ultimate aim of convincing these actors to rethink how to respond to homelessness. It will also appeal to members of the public concerned with and frustrated by the inadequacy of existing responses to homelessness.

In Chapter Two, the book explores historical and contemporary responses to homelessness, suggesting that policy and practice has, in a large part, reflected a distorted understanding of homelessness, narrowly thought of as involving males, rough sleeping and those suffering from a range of disabilities, and regarded as a source of public disorder. These distortions have arisen from research that has equated 'homelessness' with the small minority of those experiencing homelessness who sleep rough or are long-term shelter users and who do exhibit a range of disabilities, in contrast to the majority who exit homelessness relatively quickly and, other than income insufficiency or short-term adverse circumstances, do not suffer any other ailments. This distorted understanding of homelessness is also bolstered by various framings of homelessness by some advocacy groups and media, resulting in a number of myths about homelessness that are set out in the second part of the chapter.

Chapter Three then explores the empirical evidence in Ireland on the extent and composition of those experiencing homelessness in Ireland over a five-year period between June 2014 and June 2019. The number of households in emergency accommodation increased by 150 per cent over this short period and the composition changed dramatically, with families with child dependants increasingly experiencing homelessness. The single most important driver of their experience of homelessness was initially unaffordable rent increases in the private rented sector, and later the terminations of tenancies. Contrary to certain framings, rough sleeping was experienced by only a very small minority.

Chapter Four then explores the reactions by central and local governments and not-for-profit providers to this increase. The full range of standard responses was evident, from increased shelter capacity and new transitional congregate accommodation, to specific enhanced housing payments with a concomitant increase in state funding. Also evident was the growth in the number of newly formed bodies providing street-based services in Dublin in particular.

explain why people experienced residential instability, and consequently on their individual deviancy and pathology to explain their lack of participation in the labour market. As noted by Leonard (1966: 429), it was not that economic forces were unimportant or unknown, but rather that 'they generally looked elsewhere for an explanation of why the problem persisted'. Historical accounts of homelessness show that surges in homelessness are generally linked to economic depressions. For example, homelessness surged in the US in the 1930s during the Great Depression but 'the gearing up of the war machine in the early 1940s effectively winnowed the ranks of those on the streets and shelters of all but the elderly and disabled' (Hopper, 1997: 15); however, homelessness rose again following demobilisation (Hopper, 2003).

In addition, who we think of as 'homeless' has varied over time and space. As Hopper (2003: 18) observed: 'seeking to impose order on the hodgepodge of dislocation, extreme poverty, migrant work, unconventional ways of life, and bureaucratic expediency that have, at one time or another, been labelled homeless my well be a fool's errand'. This is evident in the range of terms utilised to describe this hodge-podge: 'tramps', 'hobos', 'bums', 'idle and disorderly', 'poor and indigent', 'rogues and vagabonds', 'incorrigible rogues', 'vagrants', 'idle and dissolute', 'mendicants', 'beggars', 'of no fixed abode' and so on. These terms are usually precise legal constructs or self-descriptions, for example: hobos worked and wandered; tramps wandered but did not work; bums neither worked nor wandered (Bloom, 2005); and whether you were described as a rogue or an incorrigible rogue depended on the number of convictions that you had under the Vagrancy Acts, with a third conviction labelling you an 'incorrigible rogue'.

Containing vagrants

The dominant response to managing disturbance and deviancy from the mid-19th century onwards took the form of placing these surplus populations in a range of institutions: mental asylums removed the disturbed; reformatories corrected children and inebriates; colonies confined the unemployed, vagrants and disabled; workhouses warehoused the indigent; prisons punished the deviant, and penitentiaries restored the virtue of women. Vagrancy was re-conceptualised in this period, leading to the emergence and establishment of specific congregate facilities, removing vagrants, by and large, from the realm of the prison and workhouse into dedicated facilities that married elements of the poor law and criminal law to produce persons that were 'ready' for the labour market. Those who were not amenable to participating in the labour market were placed in sites where they could be held in abeyance.

In broad terms, responses to vagrancy can be conceptualised as largely punitive from the Middle Ages, gradually being replaced by reformatory measures at the beginning of the 20th century, then overlain by a therapeutic tendency towards the second half of the 20th century, and with the provision of shelter and housing dominating the beginning of the 21st century (Maeseele et al, 2014). However, we need to be mindful that: punitive measures have always retained a residual and supporting role to reformative and inclusive approaches; therapeutic responses often conceal a punitive dimension (Gerstel et al, 1996); and punitiveness has the capacity to resurface in surprising ways in different places and at different times.

Re-conceptualising responses to vagrancy

At the end of the 19th century, the 'vagrancy question' was both a national and a transnational issue. Although there were significant national variations in approaches to managing vagrancy, with France and Germany, for example, laying much greater stress on the disabilities of vagrants than was the case in Britain, which stressed their inherent deviancy (Althammer, 2016), the International Penitentiary Congress was a key forum for discussing responses to vagrancy (Althammer, 2014). At the

Fifth International Congress in Paris in 1895, a consensus was emerging that vagrancy should be effectively removed from the penal and criminal justice realm, and that vagrancy policy should be reoriented towards rehabilitation rather than punishment. Althammer (2014) argues that this came about due to the influence of shifts in the broader penological sphere, where penal reformers were proposing penological principles based on reforming the offender, rather than the existing system of retribution in proportion to the gravity of the offence.

As vagrancy was a relatively minor offence, it tended to only attract relatively short prison sentences of a week to a month, which was deemed ineffective in deterring or curbing vagrancy and begging. Furthermore, even where harsh laws were in place, courts tended not to apply the full rigour of the law. In practice, the application of law was, at best, erratic (Althammer, 2018). The existing principles of punishment for vagrancy were based on proportionality, resulting in relatively short sentences that were viewed as not reforming the individual vagrant, deterring those considering a life of vagrancy or removing the habitual vagrant from society in order to prevent contamination. To successfully address vagrancy required indeterminate sentences that would allow for the detention of the vagrant in a specialised institution until reformed, rather than the short-term fixed sentences that were proving unsuccessful; such indeterminate sentences would also act as a deterrent to those contemplating a life of idleness and crime. In addition, it was recognised by the reformers that those who were not amenable to reformation should be detained indefinitely in order to protect society from their immediate depredations and ensure that they would not reproduce.

What spurred this debate in 1895 was that a model that embodied these reformative, deterrent and punitive principles had recently been adopted in Merxplas in Belgium in 1891. Although Merxplas was not the first or the only labour colony in continental Europe (indeed, such was the interest in vagrant colonies of various forms that Hart (1927) could produce a

15-page bibliography of published material on the subject in the 1920s), it was the fullest realisation of the application of scientific reason and best practice to manage vagrancy. It was also the most extensive colony dedicated to reforming and containing vagrants, which simultaneously embodied the contradictions and failures of successive institutional attempts to manage residential instability, as discussed later.

Being analogous in many ways to contemporary debates about the use of shelters for those experiencing homelessness (Culhane, 1992; Busch-Geertsema and Sahlin, 2007), while many observers of the continental labour colonies were rhapsodic in their support of such institutions, others were decidedly underwhelmed by the actual practice and outcomes of these colonies in comparison to the rhetoric of the promoters of such institutions. Thus, far from having a reformatory influence on vagrants and facilitating a return to society of masses of industrious workers, colonies were increasingly viewed simply as sites where vagrants could be contained and segregated from the industrious, potentially acting as a deterrent to those tempted to opt for a life of idleness due their unpleasant character and restraints.

Rethinking responses to vagrancy

By the 1930s, a move away from labour colonies was evident when, for example, the Departmental Committee on the Relief of the Casual Poor in England (Ministry of Health, 1930: 29, 30) declared that they found it 'difficult to recommend the establishment of labour colonies as a deterrent to vagrancy' and that, based on the evidence obtained from other countries, 'the reformative effect of a compulsory detention colony is very little'. While labour colonies fell out of favour, the casual wards and allied institutions associated with the Poor Laws remained in place in many European countries, surviving until the late 1960s and early 1970s.

In North America, homelessness was largely contained in specific geographical areas rather than specific institutions, albeit that the skid row areas that contained the homeless spawned a range of institutions and agencies with ambitions to salvage their souls and alleviate their apparent excessive alcohol consumption (Bibby and Mauss, 1974). The inhabitants of these institutions were surplus to labour requirements and hence the application of vagrancy laws gradually dissipated. As the relationship with the labour market declined and this surplus population was contained either within skid row in North America or various Poor Law or charitable institutions in Europe, there was neither a 'need nor rationale for disciplining them' (Hopper, 1990: 24). In addition to the hybrid criminal justice and Poor Law congregate state institutions, religiously inspired shelter services that promised salvation were prominent in the skid rows of North America and cities of Europe , albeit that they failed on a 'colossal scale' (Rooney, 1980) in achieving their objective of salvation for the homeless, simply subjecting them instead to degrading and humiliating rudimentary services.

Managing vagrant women

Contemporary accounts of homelessness for most of the 19th and 20th century focus almost exclusively on homeless men, with accounts of homeless women only emerging in the last two decades of the 20th century as part of the story of the 'new homeless'. It can be argued that women were, in fact, experiencing homelessness in large numbers in the 19th and 20th centuries (Bloom, 2005; O'Sullivan, 2016a), not just from the late 20th century, but they were rendered relatively invisible as they largely utilised a range of female-only services that were usually not formally designated as services for vagrants. Rather than using the publicly provided casual wards or privately provided lodging houses that offered communal shelter-type accommodation, women utilised a range of other sites, including convents, refuges and asylums. By focusing their attention largely on accommodation services formally designated as 'services for the homeless', investigators and enumerators concluded that the majority of those deemed homeless were male.

As a result of this methodological blindness, the small number of women found in skid row or accommodation designated for the homeless were usually described in exotic terms, often in terms of their lack of domesticity and deviant sexuality. Over the 19th and 20th centuries, economic and social pressures, particularly in a context of recurrent shortages of affordable accommodation, have generated homelessness among men and women. However, the strategies adopted by women to escape literal homelessness were more diverse than those of males, with a range of female-specific accommodation services available to them, often organised around protecting the virtue of females and the morals of society.

This thesis is supported by Althammer's (2018) work on the 'disappearance' of vagrant women from crime statistics in the second half of the 19th century. In her careful statistical analysis, she notes how the number of women arrested and prosecuted for begging and vagabondage declined from 30 per cent to 3 per cent of all prosecutions between 1870 and 1910. She argues that this was a consequence of range of charitable institutions emerging in the second half of the 20th century to provide poor relief to the deserving poor, with women deemed to be more deserving than men. This resulted in 'public and expert discourse on the vagrancy issue around 1900 [being] almost exclusively centred on the male offender' (Althammer, 2018: 745).

Welfare and vagrancy

Over the course of the 20th century, responses to homelessness gradually changed in the majority of advanced industrial countries. Responses moved from the punitive, based on an understanding of vagrancy as a source of disorder and criminality, and of indiscriminate alms giving as threatening the labour or charity contract, to largely inclusive welfare responses based on an understanding of homelessness as a form of residential instability exacerbated by a varying balance of personal and structural deficiencies. Even where vagrancy Acts were still on the statute books, they were largely redundant, particularly in Europe, and constitutional challenges in the US had formally dismantled state-level vagrancy legislation by the late 1960s, albeit that concerns over homelessness were not the key driver of these changes (Goluboff, 2016).

There is a general consensus that, while not necessarily preventing homeless, the generosity and comprehensiveness of welfare systems shape the degree to which households will experience homelessness and housing exclusion, as well as the characteristics of those households (Allen et al, 2020). The basic pattern, developed by Stephens and Fitzpatrick (2007), is that the more generous and comprehensive a welfare system, the fewer the number of households will experience homelessness, and that those households who experience homelessness will be largely single-person households and will have experienced other forms of exclusion, substance misuse and various disabilities. On the other hand, more miserly and constrained welfare systems will generate a much higher number of households experiencing homelessness, including large numbers of families, with the majority experiencing homelessness due to poverty and housing unaffordability, rather than individual-level disabilities. Evidence from two different welfare systems, the US (Kuhn and Culhane, 1998) and Denmark (Benjaminsen and Anrade, 2015), broadly confirms this pattern. Thus, while the dominant response to homelessness by the late 20th century was welfarist, different welfare regimes shaped both the scale of homelessness and the specific characteristics of those experiencing homelessness.

Despite this broadly 'inclusive turn', from the early 1980s, certain cities in the US began passing laws that prohibited sleeping in public, begging, loitering and other public space restrictions. In large part, these enactments reversed the constitutional rulings between 1965 and 1975 that limited the powers of urban authorities to criminalise vagrancy and begging, as well as the introduction of legislation that decriminalised public intoxication in 1971. This so-called 'punitive turn' was less pronounced in Europe, though Hungary is an outlier as an amendment to the Constitution in 2018 banned 'habitual residence in a public space'.

Sheltering the homeless

As the numbers of people experiencing homelessness grew from the 1980s onwards in the majority of the countries of the Global North, a model of service provision gradually evolved that saw large congregate shelters as the front-line response for people experiencing homelessness. Such shelters provided a basic humanitarian response which ensured that people were not literally on the streets – what the Americans termed 'three hots and a cot' – and also provided a place and a space to assess the needs of the person using the service in order to understand the reasons for their homelessness and what remedies were required for them to exit homelessness.

Although the popularity of congregate emergency and temporary accommodation as a response to homelessness has ebbed and flowed over the past 150 years (Hopper, 1990; Culhane, 1992; Busch-Geertsema and Sahlin, 2007), it has shown remarkable resilience, remaining a constant brooding presence and the default position for responding to periodic surges in residential instability in the Global North. In a recent review of services for people experiencing homelessness across the EU, Baptista and Marlier (2019: 77) report that:

A staircase model of service provision seems to prevail in the overwhelming majority of European Countries, i.e. in most countries the different types of support aim at assisting homeless people with their needs through different forms of temporary housing up to the point where they are ready to live independently in their own homes.

An alternative evidence-based model that provides housing first (Tsemberis, 2010) and then assists individuals with any presenting psychosocial difficulties, is gaining traction across the Global North; however, with the exception of Finland, it 'is still confined to a minority of homelessness service provision in many countries' (Pleace et al, 2019: 59; Allen et al, 2020).

As a response to homelessness, the ongoing dependence on congregate shelters in the majority of the countries of the Global North is problematic. This is because of the extensive and long-standing critiques of the limitations of this form of congregate accommodation as a response to residential instability, and the largely negative experience of those who reside in such facilities. There is no convincing evidence that the provision of large congregate shelters for people experiencing homelessness achieves anything other than a temporary, and generally unpleasant, respite from the elements and the provision of basic sustenance for people experiencing homelessness. Furthermore, for a small minority, it is an extraordinarily expensive and unsuitable long-term response to their inability to access affordable housing.

On the other hand, there is very substantial and convincing evidence that shelters impose often infantilising rules and regulations that restrict individual autonomy, allowing shelter users to survive shelter life but limiting their ability to achieve sustained exits to independent accommodation. Despite these rules and regulations, the violence and intimidation often evident in such congregate settings can result in some of the most vulnerable people rejecting entreaties to enter shelters.

However, if we think of homelessness as people sleeping rough, then our response should be to provide these people with shelter. The underlying ideology of a shelter-based response is that people should first be provided with immediate relief from their literal homelessness; then, once sheltered, a range of other services can be put in place to prepare them for housing through a series of self-improving measures, such as ensuring sobriety, abstinence from drugs and treatment for the symptoms of mental ill health, addiction, physical ill health, life-limiting illness or other disabilities.

Those that fail to meet the criteria for housing readiness – and the evidence is that this is the case for the majority of long-term shelter users – simply move between shelters, the street and other congregate residential services, without ever resolving their homelessness. In practice, it was often difficult to identify housing-ready services that conformed to all of the characteristics described earlier; however, the use of the term signalled a broad ideological disposition to understanding homelessness as resulting from various personal deficiencies that require managing and resolving prior to consideration for housing.

Managing homelessness through the provision of emergency congregate shelters is also extraordinarily expensive, and a minority of shelter users also make extensive use of other expensive emergency health services as they traverse through an 'institutional circuit' (Hopper, 1997) of short stays in various services without ever resolving their residential instability. As Hopper and Baumohl (1994: 26) argue, shelters are reactions rather than responses to homelessness as:

> demand for shelter is essentially defined by default: who appears at the door and in what numbers depend chiefly on the state of the local labour market, the supply of cheap housing, welfare regulations and sufficiency, police practices, commitment laws and practices, and the tolerance and support capacity of kin.

Rather than seeing shelters as a solution to homelessness, Hopper et al (1997: 660) have argued that 'in addition to personal "risk factors" and structural "root causes"', 'homeless service systems should be viewed as independent agents shaping the course of homelessness': where these services 'may have the perverse institutional effect of perpetuating rather than arresting "residential instability" – that is the underlying dynamic of recurring literal homelessness' – the causes of homelessness must 'also take account of the institutions that serve them'.

In the preceding short account, it is suggested that many of our historical and contemporary responses to vagrancy/homelessness were, and are, driven in large part by perceptions of vagrants and people experiencing homelessness as deviant, disreputable, drunken, disorderly and damaged – what Gowan (2010) memorably described as 'sin talk and 'sick talk'. This has resulted in the majority of countries in the Global North adopting policies and delivering services that aim to contain those who experience homelessness in a variety of generally unpleasant congregate shelters, manage their residential instability through a variety of self-improvement measures and deter them from entering emergency accommodation (politely known as gatekeeping), all of which is based on a range of stereotypes of vagrancy and homelessness.

Contemporary perceptions of homelessness

Recent research in Ireland (Crowley and Mullen, 2019) and England (Crisis, 2018) suggests that the dominant popular perception of those experiencing homelessness is that of a middle-aged man sleeping rough with addiction and/or mental health issues. Certainly, those sleeping rough are the most visible and evocative manifestations of homelessness in cities of the Global North, and indeed the majority of press stories on the topic of homelessness are usually accompanied by an image of a rough sleeper or sleepers, thus reinforcing this popular perception. Furthermore, fundraising strategies by not-for-profit bodies providing varying degrees of services to people experiencing homelessness explicitly and implicitly reinforce this perception. They do so by either using images of middle-aged males sleeping rough in their fundraising literature, or through events like sleep-outs or requests for donations of clothing and toiletries, which suggest that homelessness is equated with rough sleeping.

A striking feature of responses to homelessness in the Global North in recent years is the range of visible volunteer-led initiatives providing services that enable people to survive on the streets through the provision of mobile hygiene services, mobile health care, food and clothing (Parsell and Watts, 2017; Parsell, 2019). Much of the scientific research on homelessness has also focused on rough sleepers; again, this is not that surprising given their obvious extreme exclusion and a concern to ameliorate their distress. The persistence, and indeed the growth, of visible rough sleepers in the majority of cities in the Global North has also contributed to an erroneous perception that nothing much can be done for those people bar providing them with some level of sustenance as if their obvious distress could be alleviated, then it surely would be.

This accumulation of images and responses to homelessness has contributed to framing homelessness as, in the main, 'male', 'middle-aged' and 'rough sleeping', with the occasional appearance of eccentric women and vulnerable youth. Despite this popular perception, as discussed later, those experiencing homelessness comprise more than marginal males sleeping rough. Indeed, these marginal males sleeping rough are but a minority of those experiencing the most extreme forms of homelessness in the majority of countries of the Global North, with the exception of the US, where what they term 'unsheltered people' comprised just over one third of those experiencing homelessness at a point in time in 2018. Thus, how we imagine homelessness is shaped both by our first-hand observations and by the images, stories and discourse on homelessness. However, increasing robust data, particularly longitudinal data, are providing an analysis that fundamentally changes this perception of homelessness.

Varying experiences of homelessness

Utilising longitudinal shelter data, cluster analyses of time-series data on shelter admissions in New York and Philadelphia by Kuhn and Culhane (1998) showed a pattern whereby approximately 80 per cent of shelter users were transitional users, in that they used shelters for very short periods of time or a single episode and did not return to homelessness. A further 10 per cent were episodic users of shelters and the remaining 10 per cent were termed chronic or long-term users of shelter services. Although a relatively small percentage of single homeless people, these chronic or long-term users occupied half of all bed nights. Broadly similar findings have been replicated in studies of shelter usage in Dublin (Waldron et al, 2019), Melbourne (Taylor and Johnson, 2019), Toronto (Aubry et al, 2013) and Copenhagen (Benjaminsen and Andrade, 2015).

However, as discussed earlier, the characteristics of those in each cluster vary by the nature of the broader welfare state in which these shelters are situated. In all cases, those experiencing chronic homelessness are heavy users of criminal justice and emergency health services, and have high rates of mental health and substance abuse treatment. However, the transitional cluster in the US is largely composed of impoverished households who found themselves in emergency accommodation due to the absence of an adequate welfare safety net but have few, if any, disabilities and/or substance misuse issues. In Denmark, a generous welfare safety net ensures that few, if any, simply impoverished households enter the shelter system; however, those in the transitional cluster show similarly high rates of disabilities and/or substance misuse issues as those in the chronic cluster (Benjaminsen and Andrade, 2015).

Those who are literally homeless or sleeping rough are a small and not very representative section of those who experience homelessness either at a point in time or, more importantly, over a period of time. Research has fairly convincingly shown that in the Global North, the population of those with a long-term experience of homelessness who oscillate between the street and temporary shelters accounts for roughly 10 per cent of those who experience homelessness over time. It is thus a particularly distinctive subset of the overall population who experience homelessness over time, though one that the general population think of as 'the homeless'.

Researching the 'homeless'

A striking feature of the bulk of research on homelessness over the past 50 years is the degree to which the research has focused on those experiencing 'chronic' and 'episodic' homelessness, in many cases, long-term shelter users as well as the literal or street homeless, who are more often than not presented as 'the homeless'. Equating the 'chronic homeless' with 'homelessness' was also a consequence of the extensive use of cross-sectional research methods to research homelessness, which distorts the reality of homelessness, resulting in a truncated, decontextualised and over-pathologised picture of those experiencing homelessness by largely capturing only the chronic population (Snow et al, 1994). For Phelan and Link (1999: 1337), '[p]oint-prevalence studies focus our attention on the persistently homeless and on what is distinctive about them: factors including mental illness, substance abuse, and criminal activity'.

Equating the 'chronic homeless' with 'homelessness' has distorted how policymakers, politicians and the public understand and respond to homelessness, and this distortion has resulted in policies that fail to address the dynamics and types of homelessness. Therefore, the importance of differentiating those who experience homelessness as chronic or long term, episodic, and transitional is crucial in understanding and responding to homelessness.

For example, much of the research on homelessness and the criminal justice system has focused on the experience of those who are literally or street homeless. This is not particularly surprising as the interaction between, for example, policing and homelessness is likely to occur at the street level, but it does require careful interpretation. Thus, when describing, for example, the 'criminalisation of homelessness', the majority of the studies are, in fact, referring to the 'criminalisation of those experiencing chronic homelessness'. Equally, research on the use of health care services, such as accident and emergency services, has highlighted the disproportionate use of such services by 'the homeless', and these studies describe the often appalling health status of such individuals and their increased risk of mortality. However, as in the case of the interaction with agencies of the criminal justice system, on closer examination, 'the homeless' turn out to be largely those experiencing chronic and episodic homelessness.

In a review of studies exploring the 'prevalence of mental disorders amongst the homeless in Western Europe', the authors concluded that '[h]omeless people in Western countries are substantially more likely to have alcohol and drug dependence than the age-matched general population in those countries, and the prevalence of psychotic illnesses and personality disorders are higher' (Fazel et al, 2008: 1670). A further review of the health status of homeless people in high-income countries claimed that '[h]omeless people have higher rates of premature mortality than the rest of the population, especially from suicide and unintentional injuries, and an increased prevalence of a range of infectious diseases, mental disorders, and substance misuse' (Fazel et al, 2014: 1529). However, the studies that these reviews draw on were almost exclusively of people staying in shelters, attending soup kitchens or sleeping rough, in other words, those experiencing chronic and episodic homelessness.

With the exception of a small number of studies utilising either administrative or survey data, the 'homeless' referred to in the majority of research on the interaction between criminal and health care systems and 'the homeless' in liberal welfare regimes are primarily those experiencing 'chronic and episodic homelessness'. What is more, this research amounts to the majority of research on homelessness globally as approximately 85 per cent of published work in the English language on homelessness over the past 60 years has emanated from four liberal welfare regimes: the US, Canada, England and Australia. Furthermore, and related to the previous point, data from shelter usage and rough-sleeping enumerations, as well as interactions with other services in the Global North, all observe that the vast majority of those who are the chronic homeless/ rough sleepers are males. The reasons for this – for example, that females are more likely to be in 'hidden homeless' situations and so on (for a detailed account, see Pleace, 2016) – need not detain us here; rather, the point is to specify that chronic homelessness is largely a male phenomenon. Thus, much of the literature is, in fact, addressing males experiencing long-term homelessness resulting in a distorted understanding of homelessness and, in particular, the experience of women, who are rendered relatively invisible in such accounts. As Reeve (2018: 172) has argued: 'Homelessness is not only its visible manifestations and until this is acknowledged, homeless women will remain invisible and our understanding of the nature, character, and extent of homelessness can only be partial at best.'

Some myths of homelessness

'There but for the grace of God go I': homelessness can happen to anyone

Utilising a number of longitudinal data sets, Bramley and Fitzpatrick (2018: 112) persuasively conclude that, 'in the UK at least, homelessness is not randomly distributed across the population, but rather the odds of experiencing it are systematically structured around a set of identifiable individual, social and structural factors, most of which, it should be emphasized, are outside the control of those directly affected'. They further argue that a key predictor of homelessness is childhood poverty, with area effects also being significant, and that social support networks operate to reduce the likelihood of entering homelessness. In the case of Denmark, a comprehensive analysis of shelter use over a ten-year period shows that in a more generous welfare system, shelter use is more likely to be experienced by those with more complex needs; nonetheless, the vast majority of people, including those with mental health or substance misuse issues, are not at risk of entering shelters (Benjaminsen, 2016).

In addition, research from the US demonstrates that those using shelters and the literally homeless are growing older. This is indicative of a cohort effect, whereby the risk of experiencing homelessness and remaining homeless for disadvantaged populations is elevated for certain age cohorts as a result, for example, of entering adulthood and the labour market during economic downturns or attempting to access housing during a time of rising rental costs (Culhane et al, 2013). Therefore, the majority of households in the Global North are not at risk of experiencing homelessness, either temporarily or on a long-term basis. Rather, the risk is decisively skewed towards either those experiencing multiple social exclusions in comprehensive welfare systems such as Denmark, or those who, in particular, have experienced childhood poverty and other adversities in less generous systems, such as the UK and the US, with the timing of their entry into adulthood elevating their risk of experiencing homelessness.

'Winos': homelessness and alcohol

As Baumohl and Huebner (1991: 837; see also Stark, 1987) noted nearly 30 years ago, 'in popular, professional, and academic understandings, no condition has been so closely connected with homelessness as chronic alcohol dependence'. However, there is no conclusive research on the extent of alcohol abuse among those experiencing homelessness.

Furthermore, as the existing research is largely cross-sectional and the diagnostic tools used are problematic, such methodologies exaggerate the 'disabilities' of those experiencing homelessness. For example, one of the first comprehensive studies of alcohol and drug use among the 'homeless population' in Ireland for the National Advisory Committee on Drugs showed that of those who consumed alcohol, nearly three quarters engaged in 'harmful or hazardous drinking' (Lawless and Corr, 2005: 64). However, as the research was cross-sectional, the 'homeless population' surveyed were more likely to be those experiencing long-term chronic or episodic homelessness skewing the results. Nonetheless, individuals who engage in risky behaviour such as heavy drinking are more likely to experience homelessness than those who do not; however, this is not a given and may be more a consequence of residing in an area with tight housing markets or slack labour markets, rather than just risky consumption (Johnson et al, 2019; see also O'Flaherty, 2004 exploring the conjunction of being the 'wrong person in the wrong place'). In other words, 'alcohol and drugs are neither necessary nor sufficient causes of homelessness' (Hopper, 1989: 393).

'Bring back the asylums': disabilities and homelessness

Cross-sectional research has also consistently identified those with mental illness as being particularly vulnerable to experiencing homelessness and, indeed, part of the 'new homeless' following the period of the deinstitutionalisation of large-scale psychiatric institutions in most countries of the Global North from the 1960s onwards (Snow et al, 1986). However, in a review of research on deinstitutionalisation, serious mental illness and homelessness, Montgomery et al (2013: 68) concluded that 'the research supports there being nothing inherent to serious mental illness that leads to homelessness, rather this link is mitigated by the economic difficulties that often accompany living with mental illness in the community'.

Claims of high rates of mental illness among those experiencing homelessness arose from the limitations of the predominantly cross-sectional methodology, which 'confounded the understanding of those who became homeless with those who remained homeless' (Montgomery et al, 2013: 64).

Similarly, for Johnson et al (2019: 1107), based on their analysis of Journeys Home data (for details of this unique data set, see Wooden et al, 2012), 'those diagnosed with mental illness, another commonly stigmatised group, are less vulnerable to homelessness and their risk of becoming homeless seems unaffected by rising rents, and/or rising unemployment rates'. They speculate that this is because those with a diagnosed mental illness are likely to be receiving support services that reduce their risk of homelessness. Thus, for those with a mental illness, it seems to be the absence of supports that drives rates of entry into homelessness among this group. This has important implications for policymakers in that there is nothing intrinsic about having a disability or substance misuse issue that results in homelessness; rather, it is the absence of the necessary support services to assist such individuals to manage their disabilities or substance misuse issues in their residence that results in homelessness.

Rough sleepers: 'a wicked social problem'

The persistence of, and in some cases increase in, the number of rough sleepers in city centres across the Global North suggests that no successful response has been identified to end this acute form of exclusion; indeed, in many cases, the response was what many researchers were to describe as a punitive reaction, starting in the US but later exported to Europe and the Antipodes. From the beginning of this century, scholars and activists in the US have noted that public policy has been 'annihilating public space', making it 'impossible for homeless and other street people simply to *live* (at least without breaking any laws)' (Mitchell, 2001: 63). As a consequence, a disproportionate number of people experiencing homelessness are represented in the criminal justice system (Blower et al, 2012). This occurs because the visible homeless are 'a threat to continued accumulation and to the processes of abstract space production' (Mitchell, 2018: 109).

Others have argued for a more nuanced approach, with DeVerteuil et al (2009) arguing that while there is ample evidence of punitive approaches, other more inclusive responses are also evident, which is particularly the case when the focus shifts from the US to other jurisdictions. Johnsen and Fitzpatrick (2010) also argue that coercive policies towards the homelessness were motivated, in part, by the desire to assist service-resistant rough sleepers who were engaging in self-destructive behaviour, rather than simply vengeful actions against the powerless. The perspectives and voices of homeless people themselves are heard in a series of innovative research projects in the UK, particularly in England (for example, Johnsen and Fitzpatrick, 2010; Johnsen et al, 2018; Watts et al, 2018). In a subtle analysis, Watts et al (2018) propose an 'exacting' normative framework to judge if interventions with entrenched rough sleepers are 'effective, proportionate and balanced' and ensure their 'well-being and autonomy'.

Importantly, this framework applies to both 'hard' punitive actions, such as policing interventions, and to 'soft' tolerant interventions, such as soup runs and other services to sustain people living on the street. While acknowledging that such interventions 'raise moral and practical dilemmas' (Johnsen et al, 2018: 15), based on interviews with current and former rough sleepers, they nonetheless found that hard interventions were supported by 'homeless people themselves, especially where street lifestyles are visiting demonstrable harm on other people'.

Furthermore, in a detailed review of the research, Mackie et al (2019) have convincingly shown that assertive street outreach work coupled with the provision of suitable housing with support, that is, specific support in maintaining their accommodation *and* wider social supports, provides an effective pathway out of rough sleeping (see also Parsell et al, 2019). Conversely, in the absence of adequate support, providing short-term accommodation in unsuitable accommodation such as congregate shelters is not effective in providing a pathway out of rough sleeping. Explanations which suggest that rough sleepers are 'service resistant' are not supported by evidence. Rather, if services are oriented towards housing first in offering rapid housing, support as required and privacy, as opposed to large congregate shelters where people have had previously unsafe experiences, then there will be positive service engagement (Wusinich et al, 2019).

Charity and compassion: street services for people experiencing homelessness

In the majority of cities in the Global North, members of the public are less likely to see agents of the criminal justice system punishing those literally homeless than to witness legions of volunteers dispensing not only the traditional soup, sandwiches, tea and toiletries to them, but also increasingly a range of interventions by 'social innovators', including mobile showers and laundries. This mobilisation of care for those experiencing homelessness is transnational, and some of these services are part of this international movement to assist people experiencing homelessness. For example, Helping Handbags Dublin is part of the broader Helping Handbags body, which describes itself as 'a women's movement set up to help women who have been forced onto the streets from their homes … mostly due to the influence of alcohol and drugs within the home' (www.helpinghandbags.ie). Women are asked to locate their old handbags and fill them with 'feminine essentials like tampons, pants liners and shampoo', in addition to 'clean socks, hats, scarves and other woollies' in order that homeless women can keep warm, with the organisation aiming to collect 600 handbags in Dublin in 2019.

In addition to the direct provision of services to those on the streets, scores of fund-raising events are held across the cities of the Global North to raise funds in order to both provide these street-based services and to support other more established NGOs. One the most popular fund-raising events in recent years are sleep-outs, where people sleep out for a night in order to raise funds. Following the success of what the organisers described as the 'world's largest ever sleep out' in Edinburgh in December 2017, where 8,000 people slept out for a night, the World's Big Sleep Out organisation planned to have 50,000 people sleeping out in December 2019 across 52 cities, including Dublin, with the aim of raising US$50 million (see chapter 5 for further details).

Such gestures of solidarity with those experiencing homelessness, the efforts of legions of volunteers in a vast number of not-for-profit organisations providing a variety of services and the generosity of citizens in donating both time and money to these agencies across the Global North clearly demonstrate that people both care and are compassionate about the plight of those who are experiencing homelessness. Whether these interventions are successful in resolving homelessness or merely contain and ameliorate the worst aspects of the experience of literal homelessness by providing temporary shelter and basic sustenance is an empirical question that is, in part, addressed in the following section. In addition, the increasingly popular sleep outs, often undertaken by business leaders, may inadvertently confuse homelessness with just literal homelessness, and suggest that responses to homelessness are best done through individual acts of charity, rather than through progressive and equitable taxation and redistribution. For example, research in Ireland suggests that many people think that compassion and caring are the appropriate responses to homelessness (Crowley and Mullen, 2019), and in the case of the UK, it was reported that, in some cases, 'the public assumes that individual acts of kindness and charity towards people in crisis are effective and sufficient in addressing homelessness' (Crisis, 2018: 64).

In a series of papers, Cameron Parsell and colleagues (Parsell and Watts, 2017; Parsell, 2018, 2019) have systematically critiqued the efficacy of these caring and compassionate responses to homelessness. Parsell has argued that sympathy for those experiencing homelessness is motivated by pity, and that pity motivates this charitable and compassionate response. Such motivations also suggest that responses to homelessness should be channelled through individual acts of giving, either financially or in kind. While individual acts of kindness and compassion are well intentioned, they are *ineffective*, with research evidence suggesting that they are, in fact, *counterproductive*. Effective responses to homelessness require *housing*, not soup and sleep-outs. As argued by Parsell (2018: 94): 'the majority of services provided to people who are homeless (1) would be superfluous if we provided them with housing, (2) undermine their autonomy and well-being, (3) not only perpetuate their passive dependence but also solidify their positioning as deficient, and (4) represent our poverty of ambition'. Parsell (2019: 15) argued that homelessness can only be ended through the provision of social and affordable housing, and that these charitable and compassionate responses are distractions that are 'neither motivated by nor directed toward solving homelessness'.

Insufficient funding? Spending on homelessness

However, are these fund-raising efforts and the provision of street-based services perhaps required due to a lack of funding for services for people experiencing homelessness by governments? In a recent survey of public attitudes about homelessness in eight European countries (Petit et al, 2019), the majority (nearly three quarters) of those surveyed believed that governments were spending too little on homelessness programmes; in the case of Ireland, nearly 80 per cent believed this to be the case. A total of 60 per cent had given 'money, food or clothing' to a homeless person over the past year, and

57 per cent had given 'money, food or clothing' to an NGO or charity organisation for homeless people, with nearly 70 per cent doing so in Ireland. Equally, in a survey across 47 different US states, the majority of participants believed that the federal government should allocate more funding for those experiencing homelessness (Tsai et al, 2019). It is particularly difficult to measure the costs of homelessness. As Pleace et al (2013: 15) note, while the costs of specific services for people experiencing homelessness are usually measurable, other indirect costs, for example, the use of emergency health services, preventative services and so on, are complex to measure.

In New York, US$1.8 billion was spent in 2018 on maintaining people in shelters; in Dublin, the figure was nearly €120 million. In both Dublin and New York, this massive expenditure by city authorities on emergency accommodation has resulted in relatively low and stable rates of rough sleeping but increasingly long stays in emergency accommodation and high point-prevalence figures (see O'Flaherty, 2019; see also Chapter Three of this book). London local authorities spent over £750 million on temporary accommodation in 2017/18 (Scanlon and Whitehead, 2019). Thus, the question seems to be not how much we spend on homeless programmes, but on what programmes we spend and what outcomes we want. Nonetheless, it is clear that maintaining people in emergency accommodation is extraordinarily expensive, and the bulk of this cost is met by government funding. It is also the case that government funding and fund-raising efforts for those experiencing homelessness increase when the provision of social and affordable housing decreases.

Conclusion

In this chapter, a brief history of responding to homelessness was outlined, suggesting that policy and practice has, for the most part, reflected a distorted understanding of homelessness, narrowly thought of as males suffering from a range of disabilities sleeping rough and seen as a source of public disorder. These distortions have arisen from research that has equated 'homelessness' with the small minority of those experiencing homelessness who sleep rough or are long-term shelter users and who do exhibit a range of disabilities. This is in contrast to the majority who exit homelessness relatively quickly, and other than income insufficiency or short-term adverse circumstances, do not suffer any other ailments. These distorted understandings of homelessness were also bolstered by various framings of homelessness by some advocacy groups and media, resulting in a number of myths about homelessness. Using the example of Ireland, Chapter Three provides a detailed empirical account of the trends in, and composition of, those experiencing homelessness, allowing for a debunking of the stereotypical understanding of homelessness.

THREE

Recording homelessness

Introduction

Measuring the number of households experiencing homelessness is difficult but not impossible. Much of the difficulty relates to defining who is to be counted as experiencing homelessness. Most countries only include those literally without any form of accommodation or residing in temporary and emergency accommodation. When it comes to those in overcrowded situations, doubled up with family or friends, or in unsuitable accommodation, a small number of countries (primarily the Nordic countries) include these households in their definition of homelessness. This is often referred to as a form of housing exclusion rather than actual homelessness in that the basic norms of what constitute adequate standards of housing and the ability to make a home are absent. Whether or not to include such households may be a political decision but, in any case, difficulties exist with measuring certain forms of housing exclusion. This has resulted in rendering comparative accounts of the extent of homelessness relatively problematic (though for recent attempts, see Busch-Geertsema et al, 2014; Allen et al, 2020).

A key innovation in measuring homelessness comparatively was the development of a typology of homelessness and housing exclusion known as ETHOS by researchers at the EOH, as noted in Chapter One. This typology provides 13 categories of homelessness and housing exclusion along a spectrum of situations, ranging from being literally homeless or sleeping rough, to various forms of housing insecurity. This has allowed for reasonably accurate comparisons of *different forms* of homelessness and social exclusion across different countries, rather than *comparing total figures*, which produces wildly different numbers due to the comparative differences in defining homelessness.

In a recent review of policies for people experiencing homelessness across the EU, it was noted that 'people sleeping rough, staying in emergency/temporary accommodation services, and those living in inadequate living spaces or in places which cannot be considered "regular housing units" are the most common references used in existing definitions' (Baptista and Marlier, 2019: 12). Albeit with some caveats, this is broadly the definition used in Ireland for recording the extent of homelessness. Such a definition is often criticised for excluding households living in precarious housing conditions or doubled up and staying with family and friends. However, while 14 countries across the EU include such households in their definition of homelessness, 'only four are actually able to provide data on the extent of the phenomenon' (Baptista and Marlier, 2019: 12).

Ireland is comparatively unusual in having a national integrated bed and case management system since 2013. The Pathway Accommodation and Support System (PASS) contains information on users of emergency and temporary beds funded by the Department of Housing and local authorities. Since April 2014, data on the number and profile of households in emergency accommodation, and those in temporary and transitional accommodation – are included in the 'official' monthly figure published by the Department of Housing. Category 4 of ETHOS – residential services for those escaping gender-based violence – was included until December 2014 but was then excluded as the funding of these services was transferred from the Department of Housing to child and family services.

Although not originally designed to provide information on trends in the number of households experiencing homelessness, in the absence of alternative sources of information on the profile and extent of those experiencing homelessness, data have been extracted from PASS on a monthly basis since April 2014, providing basic stock or point-in-time data on the numbers in publicly funded emergency beds provided by either not-for-profit bodies or commercial accommodation providers, as well as their data on age, gender and household composition. The data have been criticised for excluding a number of categories experiencing housing exclusion, in particular, rough sleepers, those in accommodation services for survivors of gender-based violence and those in non-publicly funded emergency accommodation services.

Neither do these monthly data include persons who are in Direct Provision Centres (DPCs), which provide congregate accommodation with various support services for international protection applicants, who have been granted refugee status or leave to remain in Ireland by the Department of Justice/ International Protection Accommodation Service but are unable to exit Direct Provision due to their inability to secure housing. At the end of June 2019, there were 780 such persons in DPCs, or 12 per cent of the overall number in DPCs (IGEES, 2019: 22). Furthermore, at the end of June 2019, there were over 900 persons seeking international protection who, due to an increase in persons seeking international protection and constrained capacity in DPCs, were placed in commercial hotels and B&Bs by the International Protection Accommodation Service. However, while their situation is objectively identical in terms of accommodation provision to those placed by local authorities, only those placed by local authorities are counted in the monthly homeless figures.

Furthermore, there were various adjustments and modifications to the data in 2018, when approximately 600 households were removed for disputed definitional reasons; thus, the substantial increase is all the more significant given these adjustments and exclusions.

Despite these limitations, these administrative stock data do provide a timely *minimum estimate* of the extent of and, more significantly, trends in homelessness. When compared against the 2016 Census figure for homelessness, and adjusting for differences in methodology and definition, the monthly PASS figure was almost identical to the Census figure, suggesting that the PASS data are a reasonably robust, albeit imperfect, indicator of trends in the numbers in emergency accommodation in Ireland (Maphosa, 2018).

Since the first quarter (Q1) of 2014, data on the number of new adult entries to homelessness services, the number of housing and non-housing exits, the duration of stays in emergency accommodation, contacts with rough sleepers, and the number of adults with support services have been compiled on a quarterly basis in what are known as 'performance reports'. Detailed data on the expenditure on both emergency accommodation services and other interventions by service providers are also published on a quarterly basis. These data capture the contribution from both central government and local authorities (a minimum of 10 per cent) for providing services for households experiencing homelessness. Both the performance and financial quarterly reports are for clusters of three to four local authorities, known for the purposes of reporting as lead authorities. The data cited in the remainder of this chapter are derived from these reports, which are available on the Department of Housing website (see: www.housing.gov.ie/housing/homelessness/other/homelessness-data).

As noted earlier, 'homelessness and housing exclusion' is widely used across the EU not only to conceptualise those who are sleeping rough and in designated emergency accommodation, but also to include those in overcrowded and unsuitable accommodation (Busch-Geertsema et al, 2014). In the case of Ireland, data are available since 2013 via the now annual statutory assessment of what is referred to as the 'social housing needs assessment', which captures some, but not all, households experiencing housing exclusion, that is, households who qualify for social housing, with the qualification determined by income, medical need and other criteria. The number of households assessed as having a need for social housing declined by 25 per cent between 2013 and 2019, from 91,600 to 68,141.

However, as discussed in greater detail in Chapter Four, this decrease is an artefact of a change in recording practices, rather than a decline in demand for social housing tenancies. The majority of households in temporary and emergency accommodation are included in the figure of 68,141 but some non-Irish national households may not qualify for social housing due to various residency requirements, being provided with short-term emergency accommodation instead. Detailed national data are not available on the number of households who are provided with emergency accommodation but are not eligible for social housing or, strictly speaking, services for people experiencing homelessness under the provisions of the Housing Act 1988; however, in the Dublin region, one third of family households presenting as homeless and 42 per cent of rough sleepers fall into this category.

In brief, in the case of Ireland, we have a reasonably robust time series on the minimum number of adults (and their accompanying child dependants) in temporary and emergency accommodation between mid-2014 and mid-2019. Reasonably robust data are also available twice a year on the minimum number of rough sleepers in Dublin (but not outside of Dublin) on a point-in-time basis, as well as flow data on the number of rough sleepers in contact with outreach services on a quarterly basis. In a comparative context, such a timely data source is relatively rare, and despite the acknowledged limitations, it allows for an exploration of trends with a degree of accuracy that is uncommon.

Homelessness in Ireland, 2014–19

Households experiencing homelessness in temporary and emergency accommodation

The number of households in temporary and emergency accommodation funded by central and local governments in the third week of each month rose from 2,297 in June 2014 to 5,796 in June 2019, an increase of over 150 per cent. In June 2019, these households were composed of 6,497 adults and 3,675 accompanying child dependants, or 10,172 individual adults and children, up from 2,385 adults and 727 child dependants in June 2014. Two thirds of these households are accommodated in the four Dublin local authorities, and this equates to eight households per 1,000 in such accommodation in Dublin, up from three per 1,000 in 2014. If the increase in the number of households continues in the same direction as over the past five years, by 2021, it is likely that the number of households in temporary and emergency accommodation in Dublin will be close to ten households per 1,000.

In terms of household composition, just over 60 per cent of the households were single adults, with the balance made up of couples and single adults with accompanying child dependants. It is important to note that these single-person households may have child dependants or a partner but presented to homelessness services without dependants or a partner, hence their recording on PASS as 'single'. The absolute number of single-person households doubled from just under 2,000 to just over 4,000 between June 2014 and June 2019, but due to the increase in families experiencing homelessness, the percentage of single-person households has declined from over 82 per cent to 63 per cent over the same period. Three quarters were male, and single males made up 47 per cent of the overall number of households experiencing homelessness in June 2019, down from 60 per cent in June 2014. Couples with accompanying child dependants comprised just over 20 per cent in June, with the balance made up of single adults with accompanying child dependants, over 90 per cent being female.

The age profile is relatively consistent over the five years, with 60 per cent of adults aged between 25 and 44 years on average. Those aged 18–25 years declined in percentage terms from just under 18 per cent to just over 13 per cent, while those aged 45–64 years increased from just under 20 per cent to nearly 26 per cent. Those over 65 never exceed more than three per cent of the total. Female-headed households outnumber male households for those aged 18–30, with male households more likely in the older age groups, increasing for each decile but reducing again for those aged over 70.

Rough sleepers

The group most associated with homelessness in the public mind, the media and, indeed, a not-inconsiderable body of research – those who are literally homelessness or entrenched in emergency services with multiple needs – represent a very small proportion of those who have experienced homelessness in Ireland over the past five years. The vast majority of households experiencing homelessness do not sleep rough or have complex needs, as discussed later. Albeit that they are very visible, both comparatively and relative to the overall number of households experiencing extreme homelessness, the number of rough sleepers is low in Dublin, as well as outside of Dublin, with only Cork recording any significant number of rough sleepers. This seems at odds with the public perception of homelessness aided by images of homelessness presented by the media and some, but by no means all, NGOs, particularly in the fund-raising tactics utilised. Most stories on homelessness in the Irish print and broadcast media, which feature regularly due to the publication of the monthly point-in-time figures, are more often than not accompanied by an image of a rough sleeper or a dishevelled individual on the streets, often passively begging. Equally, the images used by a number of NGOs in fund-raising campaigns, particularly in the run-up to Christmas, are those of a middle-aged to older male, explicitly or implicitly presented as sleeping rough, distressed and dishevelled.

However, in contrast to the hyperinflation of the numbers in temporary and emergency accommodation, the numbers of rough sleepers, and we only have reasonably accurate and consistent point-in-time data for Dublin, have remained relatively low and stable, with a fluctuating *minimum* of between 100 and 150 individuals based on a biannual count over the past five years. The limited data available suggest that the majority are aged 18–40 years, 70–90 per cent male and a quarter to one third non-Irish nationals. However, the low number of females recorded may be a consequence of the 'strategies of invisibility' deployed by female rough sleepers, making them less likely to be recorded (Reeve, 2018: 168).

This relatively low number does not easily chime with the public perception of rough sleeping, particularly in Dublin, where large numbers of individuals are to be witnessed hunched in sleeping bags and begging in the city centre. It is likely that not all those engaged in begging during the day are sleeping rough at night; rather, they may be residing in the various city centre congregate shelters. More significantly, point-in-time data conceal the fact that a larger number of individuals sleep rough over a period of time, and we have flow data on the number of contacts with rough sleepers each quarter from the lead authorities.

For example, in Dublin during 2018 and early 2019, over 600 unique individuals who were sleeping rough were identified each quarter by street outreach teams, with nearly 70 per cent fluctuating between sleeping rough and accessing emergency shelter accommodation each quarter. Outside of Dublin, only Cork recorded any significant number of rough sleepers (at 177) in Q2 2019, with just over 70 per cent, the same percentage as in Dublin, also using emergency accommodation during that quarter. One lead authority reported eight rough sleepers in this quarter and the remaining lead authorities recorded no rough sleepers.

As noted in the introduction, the offence of being homeless was repealed by the Housing Act 1988 but other related offences were left in place, including the offence of begging. Following a judicial review of the relevant sections of the Vagrancy (Ireland) Act 1847 in 2007, it was found that the provisions were unconstitutional, and prosecutions ceased. However, the power to prosecute for begging was reintroduced under the Criminal Justice (Public Order) Act 2011. The number of recorded crime incidents of begging has fluctuated from 607 in 2012 to a high of 3,377 in 2015, dropping to 1,747 in 2018 for reasons that are unclear. Despite these relatively high numbers, in a recent survey, members of the business community in Dublin expressed their dissatisfaction with the implementation of the Act (O'Flynn, 2016). Although national-level data are not available on the nationality of those charged, in the first year of operation in Dublin, two thirds were non-Irish nationals, primarily members of the Roma community.

In addition, this population also make extensive use of other residential facilities, particularly psychiatric services (Daly et al, 2018, 2019), and non-residential services, such as accident and emergency services (Ní Cheallaigh et al, 2017). Thus, the point-in-time number of rough sleepers are but part of a larger group of residentially unstable, largely single adults who traverse an 'institutional circuit' (Hopper et al, 1997) of temporary accommodation interspersed with periods of sleeping rough. However, despite claims that the monthly point-in-time data under-represent the full extent of homelessness as they do not include rough sleepers, in fact, a significant number of individuals who periodically sleep rough are counted due to the fact that the majority access emergency accommodation at regular intervals and only a very small number do not make any use of emergency accommodation.

Ireland is comparatively distinctive in that the number of rough sleepers, or literally homeless, is relatively modest and largely concentrated in Dublin. The primary reason for the relatively low point-in-time number in Dublin is likely to stem from a combination of the massive growth in the number of shelter beds, particularly in Dublin, and the relative success of a small-scale Housing First project in Dublin (Greenwood, 2015). For example, in the same time period, the number of rough sleepers on a point-in-time basis in England increased from just under 3,000 to just over 4,500. On a point-in-time basis, in April 2019, rough sleepers in Dublin accounted for just over 3 per cent of those households in the most extreme forms of homelessness: sleeping rough and in congregate emergency accommodation.

Flows into homelessness

The number of households in temporary and emergency accommodation at any point in time is a function of the rate of entry, the rate of exit and the length of stay. Flow data are available on the rate of entry into services for those experiencing homelessness on a quarterly basis from Q1 2014 onwards. In Q1 2014, there were over 1,200 new adult entries (excluding child dependants) into homelessness services, peaking at nearly 1,800 new adult entries in Q1 2018, and dropping to nearly 1,500 in Q2 2019. For Q2 2019, this works out at just over 18 new adults *per day* entering emergency accommodation, giving an indication of the pressure that homelessness services are under to accommodate these new entries.

Existing research (Colburn, 2017) elsewhere on the flows into homelessness of families shows a seasonal pattern, whereby the number of singles increases during the winter months, while the number of families, particularly with school-age children, increases during the summer months. Possible reasons for these trends are that singles may enter shelter accommodation from literal homelessness during the winter to escape inclement weather conditions, and in the case of families, doubled-up housing situations may be tolerated during the school term but break down once schools close for the vacation period. These trends are broadly evident in the case of Ireland.

While the flow into homelessness services has eased slightly over the past year, we also have to take into account that those who entered temporary and emergency accommodation in earlier quarters remain stuck there, unable to exit to secure accommodation. Thus, in Q2 2019, there were in excess of just under 12,000 adult repeat presentations to homelessness services – adults who had entered in previous quarters and who remained in emergency accommodation – a rate of nearly 130 per day. This compares to 28 per day in Q1 2014.

The last place of residence for the majority of households with accompanying children entering emergency accommodation in each quarter in Dublin (comparable information is not available outside of Dublin) was the private rented sector or being doubled up with family or friends (Dublin Region Homeless Executive, 2019a); however, careful research tracking the last four places of residence demonstrates that those doubled up had resided in the private rented sector prior to moving in with family and friends (Long et al, 2019). Similar data are not available on the last place of residence for single-person households, but it is likely that the private rented sector and various institutional settings such as prisons, psychiatric facilities and so on would feature prominently. Thus, it is not so much the number of new entries to homelessness services each quarter that has resulted in the 150 per cent increase in households in emergency accommodation over the five years between June 2014 and June 2019; rather, it is the number of households who are unable to exit emergency accommodation that have swelled the point-in-time figure.

Length of stay in homelessness services

The number of adults in temporary and emergency accommodation for more than six months increased from just under 800 in Q1 2014 to over 3,700 by Q2 2019, an increase of 370 per cent. Nationally, 60 per cent of all shelter users were in such accommodation for more than six months at the end of Q2 2019; in Dublin, this was nearly 70 per cent, compared to just under 50 per cent in Q1 2014. Outside Dublin, nearly 45 per cent of shelter users were in emergency accommodation for more than six months in Q2 2019, compared to 26 per cent in Q1 2014. This surge in the number of adults in emergency accommodation is the consequence of the rate of new entries to homelessness services exceeding the number of exits from emergency accommodation, and has resulted in the continuous opening of new shelters for singles and increasing dependence on hotels and B&Bs for families, alongside the opening of nearly 30 congregate facilities for families.

More detailed information is available for the Dublin region, which shows that the number of households with accompanying child dependants in emergency accommodation for more than 18 months increased from 919 to 1,257, or from 7 per cent to over 27 per cent of such households, between September 2016 and June 2019 (Morrin, 2019). In the case of single adults, in June 2019, nearly 800, or one third of all singles, were in emergency accommodation for more than 18 months, compared to 679 in June 2018.

Exiting homelessness

The number of adults exiting emergency accommodation to social housing, either via a social housing tenancy or with social housing support in the form of various rent supplements, has fluctuated by quarter, but in Q2 2019, nearly 1,000 adults exited to such accommodation. Between Q1 2014 and Q2 2019, over 15,000 adults exited emergency accommodation, albeit that some may have returned to emergency accommodation over the same period. Just over one third of these housing exits were to a social housing tenancy managed by a local authority or a not-for-profit AHB, with the remaining obtaining housing in the private rented sector; in nearly all cases, this was with the assistance of the Homeless Housing Assistance Payment (HAP), a housing allowance that provides enhanced rates for households at risk of experiencing homelessness or seeking to exit emergency accommodation, as explained in greater detail in Chapter Four. Reliance on exits via the private rented sector has grown over this period. For example, in the case of Dublin, just over 70 per cent of all exits to housing in the first half of 2019 were to the private rented sector, via Homeless HAP in virtually all cases, compared to 50 per cent in the first half of 2014.

Others exited from emergency accommodation to stay with friends, migrated, entered other services such as hospital or, in a few cases, were imprisoned; however, such exits are inherently unstable and many return to emergency accommodation. Each local authority can pay deposits and advance rental payments for any households in emergency homeless accommodation. This large flow of exits from emergency accommodation explains why the point-in-time monthly figure has not increased as dramatically as the flows into emergency accommodation would predict. However, on a daily basis, the number of new entries to emergency accommodation exceeded the numbers exiting to secure tenancies for each quarter from 2014 to Q2 2019, hence the gradual increase each month in the point-in-time figure. For example, in Q2 2019, there was an average of just over ten adult exits from homelessness to housing each day but there were 16 new adult entries. Hence, the HAP response to homelessness has achieved considerable success in facilitating exits from emergency accommodation to tenancies, some more secure than others, but not at the rate required to reduce the point-in-time monthly figure due to the continuous and higher rate of entries into emergency accommodation.

More detailed information is available on the number of households with and without accompanying child dependants who exited homelessness services in Dublin. Between June 2014 and June 2019, nearly 4,500 households with accompanying child dependants entered homelessness services, a total of 5,500 adults and 8,500 accompanying child dependants. In the third week of June 2019, there were just under 1,800 households in temporary and emergency accommodation in Dublin, up from 350 in June 2014. Thus, over the period in question, 60 per cent of the households that had entered emergency accommodation had exited by June 2019, albeit not all to tenancies.

In the case of single adults with accompanying child dependants, approximately 7,800 entered emergency accommodation between June 2014 and June 2019, with 2,570 in emergency accommodation on the third week in June 2019, up from 1,200 in June 2014. This suggests that nearly 70 per cent of single adults who entered emergency accommodation over this period had exited by June 2019.

Further information is available on the nearly 3,000 households with accompanying child dependants who entered emergency accommodation between 2016 and 2018. By July 2019, half had exited to tenancies, 30 per cent remained in emergency accommodation and no information was available on the remaining 20 per cent. Of those households who exited to a tenancy, just over half entered a HAP tenancy and the balance exited to an AHB or local authority tenancy. Significantly, over the three years, exits to HAP increased from 38 per cent in 2016 to 77 per cent in 2018, once again illustrating the increasing dependence on the private rental market to secure exits from emergency accommodation. Households exiting to HAP tenancies over this period spent, on average, considerably less time in emergency accommodation than those who exited to an AHB or local authority tenancy; however, this may be due to the greater volume of availability of HAP tenancies than social housing tenancies (Morrin, 2019).

Outside Dublin, there were approximately 6,700 exits from emergency accommodation to social housing tenancies or supports (data on the household composition of those exiting to housing are not available outside of Dublin), with just over

2,100 adults in emergency accommodation in June 2019, implying that nearly 70 per cent exited emergency accommodation over this period.

However, single-person households, particularly those with support needs, and households with large numbers of child dependants face difficulties exiting. This is a consequence of the limited number of social housing tenancies available for singles as much of the stock is three-bedroom units, and because the proposed number of units to be made available via a Housing First programme (see Chapter Four) does not meet the identified demand. Households with a large number of child dependants face barriers exiting via social housing supports due to both limited availability and a preference by private landlords for smaller households; additionally, as with singles, the number of social housing tenancies available is inadequate to meet demand. Despite the relentlessly increasing monthly point-in-time figure of households in temporary and emergency accommodation, it is worth noting that some 15,000 adults exited from this form of accommodation over the past five-and-a-half years.

A changing landscape

Not just Dublin

As noted earlier, one third of households in temporary and emergency accommodation are outside of the four local authorities in Dublin, where the number nearly tripled between June 2014 and June 2019. However, the four other large urban authorities in Ireland – Cork, Galway, Limerick and Waterford – have seen a doubling of households in emergency accommodation. Moreover, in the other more rural areas, the numbers increased from 359 adults to nearly 1,100 from June 2014 to June 2019. The rate of increase is broadly similar throughout the country; thus, the percentage of homeless adults outside Dublin has remained constant since data collection commenced in June 2014. However, in June

2019, there was nearly the same number of adults in emergency accommodation outside of Dublin as there was in the country as a whole in June 2014. This increase is posing considerable challenges in providing an adequate response as local authorities in many rural areas had, until very recently, few people experiencing homelessness and hence very limited services, with many tending to encourage people experiencing homelessness to gravitate to the larger urban areas where an infrastructure of services existed. Such transfers are now strongly resisted by urban local authorities and, as discussed later, rural authorities are increasingly dependent on hotels and B&Bs to meet need at a considerable financial cost. Thus, rather than being primarily an urban issue, households experiencing homelessness are increasingly found in all parts of Ireland, though the type of service available varies significantly.

Families experiencing homelessness

In terms of household composition, in June 2019, 63 per cent of people experiencing homelessness nationally were single adults with no accompanying child dependants, 22 per cent were couples with accompanying child dependants and the remaining 15 per cent were single adults, overwhelmingly female, with accompanying child dependants. The number of child dependants accompanying their parent(s) in temporary and emergency accommodation was over 700 in June 2014, though this increased by over 400 per cent to nearly 3,700 in June 2019. Thus, households with accompanying child dependants now comprise nearly 40 per cent of households experiencing homelessness and residing in emergency accommodation. When data collection commenced in June 2014, over 80 per cent of households in emergency accommodation were single; thus, a striking feature of the recent Irish experience is the growth in families experiencing homelessness.

More detailed information is available for Dublin on the number of families entering emergency accommodation for the first time per month, commencing in January 2013 when five families entered emergency accommodation. This figure has risen relentlessly since then, albeit with some seasonal variation, as noted earlier, and now regularly exceeds 100 entries per month. The highest figure recorded to date was in July 2018, with 122 new entries to emergency accommodation. Also in Dublin, a cluster analysis of households in emergency accommodation between 2012 and 2016 showed that families were considerably more likely than singles to be categorised as chronic due to their length of time in emergency accommodation, at 25 per cent compared to 9 per cent, respectively. However, they still spent considerably less time in emergency accommodation (at 407 nights) than did chronic singles (at 809 nights) (O'Donoghue-Hynes et al, 2018). Family homelessness is generally quite different from homelessness among single adults; first is the extent to which family homelessness is experienced by women; and, second, family homelessness is not characterised by high rates of complex support needs, such as addiction and severe mental illness, as can be the case for single adults experiencing recurrent and sustained homelessness (Baptista et al, 2017).

Gender and homelessness

This increase in families experiencing homelessness has contributed to a growing awareness of gender in homelessness in Ireland; however, the number of single adult females has also doubled over the same period, from 529 to 1,054, or just over 18 per cent of all households experiencing homelessness. In June 2019, there were over 2,300 females-headed households in temporary and emergency accommodation, compared to just over 800 in June 2014, an increase of 190 per cent; male-headed households increased by 130 per cent over the same period.

Both Irish (Mayock et al, 2015) and comparative evidence (Pleace, 2016; Bretherton, 2017) suggests that enumerating only rough sleepers and those using shelters and hotels will significantly underestimate the extent of homelessness and exclusion among women. A notable feature of the recent Irish experience is the growth in the number of women experiencing homelessness despite the restricted definition used, with female-headed households accounting for 40 per cent of all adults in emergency accommodation in June 2019. Furthermore, if those female-headed households in residential facilities for those who have experienced gender-based violence were included in these data, as they had been up until January 2015, this figure would be even higher.

Hotels and B&Bs

In April 2014, there were just over 800 adults experiencing homelessness in hotels/B&Bs, in the absence of other forms of emergency accommodation generally referred to as Private Emergency Accommodation (PEA), with 95 per cent of those in Dublin. By June 2019, the number of adults in PEA increased by over 300 per cent to 3,274, which exceeded the numbers in congregate emergency and temporary accommodation provided by the not-for-profit sector for the first time since the data were collected in April 2014. In the case of Dublin, just over half of the accompanying child dependants were also in PEA (data are not available outside of Dublin). Despite a number of initiatives to lessen dependency on what is universally recognised as inappropriate and unsuitable accommodation for households experiencing homelessness, dependence on such forms of accommodation has grown month on month over the past five years. The fact that more than half of all adults in emergency accommodation are in PEA is a dramatic change in service provision over a short period of time.

Migration

Of the 6,020 adults and children recorded as homeless in the 2016 Census (excluding missing cases), just over 14 per cent were non-Irish (Grotti et al, 2018). In the case of Dublin (no published data are available outside of Dublin), Irish nationals comprised nearly 90 per cent of adults in emergency accommodation in 2014, though this had declined to 67 per cent by 2018. This appears to be accounted for by the increase in the number of households with accompanying child dependants, of which a large number are non-Irish households who had lived for long periods of time in the private rented sector but through either their tenancy being terminated or their rent being increased to unaffordable levels have found themselves in emergency accommodation (Long et al, 2019). Non-Irish nationals with child dependants comprised nearly 40 per cent of all households newly accessing emergency accommodation in 2018. There is also a group who are awaiting residency status who are being provided with emergency accommodation, initially on a night-by-night basis but now on a more long-term basis, due to the lack of clarity as to whether they are entitled to social housing support or tenancies. Thus, the increase in the point-in-time data of non-Irish nationals may reflect the difficulty that some such households encounter in exiting emergency accommodation in the absence of social housing supports.

Traveller households

The 2016 Census recorded that of the 6,871 adults and children in emergency accommodation, 517 (7.5 per cent) were Irish Travellers, despite the fact that Irish Travellers comprise only 0.7 per cent of the general population. In a recent review of Traveller accommodation, an independent expert group noted that 9 per cent of all families in emergency accommodation in Dublin in late 2018 were Travellers, and that these families had an average of 2.65 accompanying child dependants (Expert Group, 2019). Although detailed data are not available outside of Dublin, the Expert Group (2019: 14) noted that 'some research exists which suggests this is a significant problem in other regions'. The Expert Group (2019: 7) also noted that based on the 2016 Census, 'the average Traveller household size was 5.3 persons (compared to 2.75 persons for the general population) and more than one in four Irish Traveller households had six or more persons, compared with less than one in twenty households in the State overall'. Thus, it is likely that the larger-than-average family size of Traveller households restricts their ability to exit emergency accommodation through securing accommodation in the private rented sector via social housing supports or tenancies in the social housing stock due to a mismatch between the type and size of dwellings available and family size, resulting in the increase of Traveller households in emergency accommodation. This is particularly the case in the four Dublin local authorities, where, for example, there were in excess of 10,000 HAP recipients at the end of 2018 but only 21 Traveller households in receipt of the payment, which has become the most significant social housing support option for both preventing and exiting homelessness (as will be documented in greater detail in Chapter Four).

In the case of both non-Irish national families and Traveller households, data on the flow of such households into emergency accommodation, in addition to the point-in-time data, are required to understand the dynamics of their experience of homelessness. As point-in-time data may distort and exaggerate such households' experience of using emergency accommodation, flow data would clarify whether such households are at greater risk of entering emergency accommodation, and hence their greater presence at a point in time, or whether they are at greater risk of getting 'stuck' in emergency accommodation due to a mismatch between household composition and the available stock of housing, or the lack of eligibility for social housing supports. The disproportionate number of Traveller and non-Irish households in emergency accommodation at a point in time is more likely to be a reflection of the structural and legal barriers to exiting emergency accommodation than any propensity for such households to access emergency accommodation.

Complex needs?

The popular perception of those experiencing homelessness is that they have complex needs due to their high levels of disabilities and/or substance misuse as discussed in Chapter Two, and hence face significant difficulties in exiting emergency accommodation and securing independent accommodation. However, in an exploration of patterns of shelter use in Dublin between 2012 and 2016, long-stay shelter users, who comprised 12 per cent of all users, occupied 50 per cent of all bed nights. A further group of episodic users who used shelters intermittently accounted for 10 per cent of shelter users, using 15 per cent of bed nights. Thus, 22 per cent of shelter users – the chronic and episodic – accounted for 65 per cent of all bed nights between 2012 and 2016 (Waldron et al, 2019). This demonstrates that the vast majority of those who used shelter beds in Dublin during this period exited their emergency accommodation relatively quickly and did not return, which implies that they did not have any significant psychosocial difficulties; rather, they had a temporary loss of secure accommodation but this residential instability was resolved relatively quickly.

Other more recent data support the view that it is the inability to retain or secure accommodation rather than psychosocial issues that characterises the transitional cluster in Dublin. Nearly three quarters of adult exits to tenancies in Q2 2019 did not require any on-site settlement support, compared to 30 per cent in Q1 2014. In this relatively short time period, not only did the number of adult exits to tenancies increase from just under 150 in Q1 2014 to over 900 in Q2 2019, but the majority of adults did not require any assistance, other than enhanced rent support, to exit and maintain their tenancy. This strongly suggests that income insufficiency, rather than any complex needs or individual-level deficiency, is the major barrier to exiting emergency accommodation. That the vast majority of families who exited emergency accommodation to tenancies did not return to emergency accommodation (Morrin, 2019: 21) reinforces this understanding of homelessness as resulting from an inability to retain accommodation in the private rented sector due to the terminations of tenancies and difficulties in securing alternative accommodation due to a lack of supply.

Ireland in comparative perspective

As noted at the beginning of this chapter, comparing the extent to which people experience homelessness across different countries requires considerable caution due to definitional issues. In the case of Ireland, only the first three categories of the ETHOS typology are regularly recorded that is, those literally homeless (only for Dublin), those in emergency accommodation and those in temporary and transitional accommodation. It is possible to compare the number of households in these categories for a number of other European countries, including Denmark and Finland. In the case of Demark, the number of households in the first three categories of ETHOS rose by 12.5 per cent, from 3,240 to 3,647, between 2013 and 2019 on a point-in-time basis, or from 1.4 to 1.5 households per 1,000 households. In Finland, the number of households declined by just over 44 per cent between 2013 and 2018, or from .06 to .03 households per 1,000 households (for further details, see Allen et al, 2020). Thus, using this restrictive definition of homelessness, the Irish experience over the past five years or so is distinctive, with significantly higher rates of increase, in absolute numbers and per 1,000 households, in the number of households experiencing homelessness on a point-in-time basis than in countries where comparable data are available.

Conclusion

In a relatively short period of time, the number of households in emergency and temporary accommodation rapidly increased in Ireland. Although regular criticisms have been made of the limitations of the PASS data due to various exclusions (for example, Daly, 2019), the data provide a minimum estimate of the extent of households experiencing the most acute forms of homelessness, and the broad trend and profile of those experiencing homelessness is clear. Based on these data, those experiencing homelessness are largely aged under 45, increasingly female-headed households and with a significant increase in adults with accompanying child dependants. The number of single adults, both males and females, is declining as an overall proportion of all households experiencing homelessness, but they still account for nearly two thirds of households in emergency accommodation.

The majority of those who enter emergency accommodation will exit to tenancies but not at a fast enough pace to reduce the monthly point-in-time number in emergency accommodation. However, that so many can exit, with the majority simply requiring financial support to access the private rented sector, rather than support for psychosocial issues, shows that housing insecurity and unaffordability are the most significant drivers of this observed increase in households experiencing homelessness.

Thus, in this short time frame, not only has there been a dramatic increase in households experiencing homelessness, but the profile of these households and their pathways into homelessness has disrupted popular perceptions of homelessness as the preserve of single older males with disabilities and addictions sleeping rough. Although earlier data are scant and unreliable, the evidence suggests that in the last decades of the 20th century, those who experienced homelessness – or, more accurately, those in emergency accommodation or sleeping rough – were primarily male, single and Irish born.

Based on current trends, for example, the numbers of female-headed households, both singles and with accompanying child dependants, with or without a partner, will increase over the next number of years, indicating a radically different picture of homelessness in Ireland than prevailed in the recent past. Thus, homelessness in early 21st-century Ireland is of a very different hue than prevailed for much of the 20th century.

This increase and change in profile of those experiencing the most acute forms of homelessness does not mean that we are all equally at risk of experiencing homelessness; rather, as highlighted earlier, it is already-disadvantaged households that are most likely to be unable to withstand the price pressures in the private rented sector, or when tenancies are terminated, and least likely to have the support networks that protect other households from experiencing homelessness. In addition, recent migrants and Traveller households also face a heightened risk of experiencing homelessness. The pool of people experiencing homelessness has expanded in recent years but it remains a pool of disadvantaged households. Nonetheless, this change in profile does require changes in how we think about homelessness, as well as the nature of our response, which is the subject of Chapter Four.

FOUR

Reacting to homelessness

Introduction

This chapter explores the policy and practice responses to households experiencing homelessness in Ireland, focusing on the period from 2016 to mid-2019. As noted in the previous chapter, very few other countries have experienced such a dramatic increase in homelessness in such a short space of time; thus, it allows for a detailed exploration, in a comparative context, of how policymakers respond in such circumstances.

This chapter analyses the various reactive measures to the increasing number of households presenting to homelessness services. In earlier responses to homelessness, there was an ideological core to the response in that those experiencing homelessness required rehabilitation and redemption, and congregate facilities were geared towards achieving this goal.

Although elements of this response remain, the current policy is best described as *reacting to homelessness* via a series of ad hoc interventions that are designed to minimise and mitigate the impact of housing instability and resultant homelessness on families and individuals, rather than address the drivers of homelessness. Many of the newly devised interventions around prevention described in this chapter, such as enhanced rent allowances to allow households access to the private rented sector and extending the shelter system, have contributed to moderating the flow into homelessness and keeping the numbers sleeping rough, or literally homeless, relatively low, as documented in Chapter Three. However, while valuable in their own right for the individuals and families concerned, these reactions to homelessness do not resolve the primary determinant of the residential instability experienced by those presenting to homelessness services: the housing affordability and accessibility crisis.

The affordability crisis manifests itself in spiralling rents in the private rented sector that price out welfare-dependent households, despite the increase in the rent allowances, and provides a rationale for landlords to terminate tenancies in order to command higher market rents. The crisis in accessibility is demonstrated in the demand for secure social housing massively outstripping the supply. These crises are not unique to Ireland, nor are they just a consequence of the Global Financial Crisis; rather, they are the result of longer-term trends in the commodification of housing. These trends are evident in the majority of the countries of the Global North, and the Irish example is a microcosm of these international trends intensifying residential instability.

The direction of housing policy

Rebuilding Ireland

Published in 2016 by the Department of Housing, Planning, Community and Local Government, *Rebuilding Ireland* is the most recent iteration of homelessness policy in Ireland, aimed at providing 'an urgent response to the homeless crisis' (for details on the various strategies pre-2016, see Allen et al, 2020; and O'Sullivan, 2008 and 2016b). In contrast to earlier strategies that had aimed to end homelessness by a particular date, as noted in Chapter One, no specific commitment to ending homelessness was given in *Rebuilding Ireland*. Rather, it contains a series of actions primarily designed to enhance the coordination of services, particularly across statutory bodies; among others, such actions were to provide over 650 tenancies in a national Housing First Programme and to deliver 1,000 rapid-build units. *Rebuilding Ireland* contains five pillars or policy domains (addressing homelessness, accelerate social housing, build more homes, improve the rental sector and utilise existing housing), with each pillar focusing on specific aspects of the housing crisis with a series of actions and specific timelines. For example, the Homelessness Pillar contains 38 actions, 31 of which were deemed to have been completed at the end of Q1 2019.

The outstanding ongoing actions included the provision of temporary modular homes for families experiencing homelessness, expanding Housing First nationally, accelerating the rapid-build housing programme, the development of a homelessness prevention strategy for non-Irish nationals without entitlements and plans to deny accommodation for a period of up to five years to households who have refused two 'reasonable offers' of social housing in a 12-month period. That the vast majority of actions specifically in relation to responding to homelessness in *Rebuilding Ireland* are deemed complete by the Department of Housing, Planning, Community and Local Government suggests that the policy has achieved the stated objective of 'providing an urgent response to the homeless crisis' (https://rebuildingireland.ie/address-homelessness/). However, as detailed in Chapter Three, the number of households in temporary and emergency accommodation grew continuously after the publication of *Rebuilding Ireland*.

How, then, do we explain the increase in households experiencing homelessness when the majority of the actions designed to respond to the crisis have been implemented? It is partly explained by interpreting the Homelessness Pillar as a series of ad hoc reactions to dimensions of homelessness, rather than a coherent and integrated strategy. All the actions are useful in themselves but they mainly address only sections of the population experiencing homelessness, for example: Housing First for a minority of those experiencing long-term homelessness; clarifying the legal obligation to non-Irish nationals; providing additional shelter beds and funding for singles and families, including pregnant women; penalising those households who do not accept 'reasonable offers' of accommodation, primarily in the private rented sector; and additional funding for substance misuse and mental health services. However, in stemming the flow of households into emergency accommodation and facilitating the speedy exit of those households who do enter emergency accommodation, the *Rebuilding Ireland* pillars or policies on social housing and the private rented sector are particularly crucial.

Of the 31 actions in relation to the Social Housing Pillar, 19 were deemed complete in Q1 2019, with the remaining actions ongoing or on schedule; in relation to the Private Rented Sector Pillar, of the 54 actions identified, 32 were deemed complete, with 22 ongoing or on schedule. As earlier, we are left with the paradox of increasing numbers of households in emergency accommodation despite the successful completion of the majority of actions designed to resolve homelessness and to enhance access to tenancies in social housing and the private rented sector.

The pillars of *Rebuilding Ireland* on the provision of social housing and the private rented sector, as with the pillar on homelessness, provide a range of very helpful measures, including additional funding for social housing and a rebalancing from the acquisition of stock to the building of stock by local authorities, as well as provisions in the private rented sector to professionalise the sector, increase notice periods for the terminations of tenancies and introduce rent pressure zones to moderate rent increases. However, as with the actions on homelessness, while useful in their own right, these changes do not fundamentally disrupt the structural failings of the system.

As we saw in Chapter Three, the data on the trajectories of families in emergency accommodation is conclusive that they are via the private rented sector, where tenancies are being terminated perfectly validly for various reasons under the provisions of the Residential Tenancies Acts 2004–19. That landlords can validly terminate a tenancy and demand vacant possession if they wish to sell the property, refurbish the dwelling or give it to a family number are not addressed in *Rebuilding Ireland*, and actions are needed to rebalance the private property rights of landlords with the needs of households for the secure occupancy of their rental dwellings.

Rebuilding Ireland aims to provide 138,000 units of social housing over the period 2016–21. The majority (63 per cent) will be social housing supports, with 'build' accounting for 24 per cent, acquisitions 5 per cent and leasing 7 per cent. The category 'build' includes new social housing constructions by local authorities and AHBs, properties acquired from private developers as part of their legal obligations, and returning local authority units that were void for various reasons to use. Therefore, the traditional method of responding to social housing need – local authorities building housing to rent to qualified households – has shrunk. In the first three years of *Rebuilding Ireland*, just over 3,300 units of social housing were *built* by local authorities, or 30 per cent of the 'build' output.

Social housing tenancies and social housing supports

The decline in local authority social housing output noted in the introduction to the book, while exacerbated by the Great Recession, was a long-term trend whereby the provision of social housing was moving from a bricks-and-mortar approach to a rent subsidy-based approach (see Hayden, 2014; Norris and Byrne, 2017). The most significant change in the provision of subsidised housing in Ireland was the introduction of housing benefit or demand-side subsidies by local authorities. Two different schemes were introduced: initially, the Rental Accommodation Scheme (RAS) in 2004; then, and more significantly, the HAP in 2014, which was outlined in Chapter

Three. The HAP allows qualified applicants to rent from the private market through the local authority paying the full market rent to the private landlord, while the tenants pay an income-related rent to the local authority. A third scheme operated by the Department of Social Protection since 1977, known as Rent Supplement (RS), where the gap between the market rent and the tenant's income was provided to the tenant, is being phased out; both RS and RAS will be fully replaced by HAP over the next few years.

The introduction of both RAS and HAP, in which households are accommodated in private rented accommodation with the majority of their rent being paid by the local authority, has resulted in a drift from providing social housing directly via construction by local authorities and AHBs to discharging their obligations with what has been termed 'social housing supports' provided by private providers. As these schemes are conceptualised as 'long-term social housing supports', the recipients of these payments are deemed to have their housing needs met, as noted in Chapter Three in relation to the number of households assessed as having a 'housing need' (Corrigan and Watson, 2018). However, it has also opened 'social housing' to significantly more households than was the case in the past. As Lewis (2019: 147) has noted: 'open access to supported housing for most newly formed households is only tempered by the availability of private rented accommodation and the lingering influences of a dualist housing mentality that discourages some from applying for social housing'.

While a HAP social housing support is, in theory, substantially quicker to access than a social housing unit provided by a local authority or AHB as a significant 'queue' exists for social housing tenancies, in effect, it is nonetheless a private rented sector tenancy. By mid-2019, just under 90,000 households (approximately 25 per cent of all households living in the private rented sector) were collectively in receipt of one of the three housing benefits to support their private rented tenancy, at a cost of just under €600 million in 2018. At the end of 2018, there were approximately 178,000 units of social housing, approximately 10 per cent of the housing stock, provided by either a local authority or AHB, with tenants paying an income-related rent, rather than cost–related rent, requiring an indirect subsidy of approximately €700 million. However, the key significant difference between the two forms of rent subsidy is that those tenants of social housing have de facto security of tenure, with an extremely low number of terminations of tenancy, whereas those in receipt of social supports have relatively weak security of tenure.

Despite the increase in supply of both social housing tenancies and social supports, there were just over 68,000 households assessed as qualified for housing support as of June 2019, a decrease of nearly 23,000 households on the 2016 figure. This drop reflects not a decrease in objective need for social housing, but a policy decision to treat those households in receipt of a HAP payment as having their social housing needs met. Tenants in receipt of earlier forms of RS were entitled to remain on the housing waiting list but this is not the case for HAP recipients. Including the nearly 48,500 households in receipt of a HAP payment in June 2019, which would be broadly comparable with the criteria for inclusion on the housing waiting list that prevailed until 2014, would have seen an increase of nearly 27,000 households, rather than the reduction reported earlier.

In a byzantine administrative procedure, recipients of HAP can be placed on a 'transfer list' to be provided with 'social housing' rather than a 'social housing support', leading the Oireachtas (Houses of Parliament) Joint Committee on Housing, Planning and Local Government (2018: 6) to caustically note that 'HAP tenants are categorised as both housed and in need of housing'. National level data on the number of households on these 'transfer lists' is not published, and we do not therefore know how many households who are deemed to have had their housing needs met via the HAP scheme can still have their preferred choice of a social housing tenancy met via an opaque 'transfer list'.

Housing policy for households unable to afford market rents or to purchase their own dwelling has been in gradual transition over the past three decades but the new model of provision is now becoming more visible. The provision of social housing supports has increasingly replaced the provision of social housing tenancies, albeit that social housing tenancies continue to be provided but at a much reduced rate compared to much of the 20th century. Social housing supports have increased access for households who would not traditionally have sought social housing, and provide alternatives to the mono-tenurial social housing estates that dominated provision in the 20th century. Although the provision of mono-tenurial social housing estates appears to have fallen out of favour, largely due to a perception that such estates were a failure and beset with social problems, the empirical evidence shows that '[s]ome social housing fails and provides poor living environments for residents but most of it succeeds' (Norris and Fahey, 2014: 219). For the majority of households in emergency accommodation, or at risk of entering emergency accommodation, a social housing support is the only option given the limited supply of social housing tenancies and the length of time required to acquire such a tenancy due to massive demand relative to supply.

Providers and services

In 2019, just over 50 different non-governmental agencies were funded by central and local government to the tune of nearly €100 million to provide just over 280 discrete services for people experiencing homelessness, the majority of which are congregate residential services. Four NGOs account for nearly 60 per cent of this state funding, and these same four NGOs were also in receipt of approximately €30 million generated from fund-raising campaigns and donations.

A myriad of private for-profit bodies operating hotels and B&Bs have a predicted budget of nearly €95 million for 2019 to provide temporary and emergency accommodation, largely for families. In addition, local authorities provide a range of administrative services, including Place Finders staff (who assist households to locate accommodation) and other allied non-residential services, with a budget of €14 million in 2019.

A range of other services, including a small number of congregate shelters, as well as a host of street-level providers of tea, toiletries, clothing, soup and sandwiches, operate without any state funding, though many have very active fund-raising campaigns, for example, Inner City Helping the Homeless, one of the most visible and vocal of the street-based services in Dublin, received €225,000 in donations in 2017.

Until recently, temporary and emergency accommodation for people experiencing homelessness was provided almost exclusively by not-for-profit bodies, with only Dublin City Council providing any direct emergency accommodation, and hotels and B&B-type accommodation utilised relatively rarely. In addition to long-term supported accommodation services, temporary and emergency accommodation services are now almost exclusively provided by either not-for-profit agencies or commercial for-profit entities, with no local authority providing any direct temporary or emergency accommodation provision. In the absence of any statutory body providing emergency accommodation services, the provision of emergency accommodation for the increasing number of households experiencing homelessness is dependent on the activities of not-for-profit bodies increasingly dominated by a small number of providers, as well as an array of accommodation providers, whose primary objective is commercial and not the provision of services for those experiencing homelessness.

Until recently, the majority of NGOs that provided accommodation and allied services for people experiencing homelessness received a generally discretionary and inadequate grant from health and social services or local authorities to assist in the running of their services. For example, during the late 1980s, the Galway Simon Community, one of the two agencies involved in managing the shelter that I worked at, received a grant from the health services of just over €29,000 per annum to part-fund their work in the shelter, as well as the running of a small, long-term residential facility. In more recent years, services for those experiencing homelessness are identified by local authorities and put out for public tender. This has both intensified competition between NGO service providers and, due to the apparent practice of awarding the tender on the basis of the lowest price, may result in services that are deemed to be required by the local authorities being subsidised by NGO providers from income generated through fund-raising and donations. The implications of this model of funding have not been fully explored, but information is required at a practice level on the implications for the capacity of organisations to deliver quality services if cost is the overriding factor in awarding tenders, as well as at a policy level on the implications of the growing dependence by the state on a relatively small number of NGOs to deliver services and implement policy.

Hotels and hubs

As noted in Chapter Three, from the beginning of the decade, the use of hotels and B&B-type accommodation increased nationally, with nearly 3,300 adults in such accommodation in mid-2019, compared to just over 800 in mid-2014. The cost of utilising hotels and B&Bs in the first half of 2019 was a staggering €2 million per week, (€1.5 million in Dublin and €0.5 million outside of Dublin), compared to just over €200,000 per week in the first half of 2013. Hotels and B&Bs are, at best, able to meet short-term, not long-term, accommodation needs, and their unsuitability across a range of domains for families experiencing homelessness, both short and long term, is both well documented and uncontested (see, for example, Hearne and Murphy, 2018; Nowicki et al, 2019). Indeed, the negative experience for families, and particularly their accompanying child dependants, is the most documented aspect of contemporary homelessness in Ireland.

In an effort to reduce the use of these forms of emergency accommodation, congregate transitional accommodation units were established, known as Family Hubs, managed primarily by not-for-profit bodies but with some private sector providers. The first Family Hub opened in Dublin in late 2016, and by mid-2019, there were 28 such facilities across the country, the majority of them (22) in Dublin, with plans in train to provide additional Family Hubs. By mid-2019, they had a capacity for 659 families, providing varying levels of in-house services at a projected revenue cost of nearly €24 million for 2019. The development of these Family Hubs was not underpinned by any evidence as to their efficacy. The research evidence is clear that both long- and short-term housing subsidies are considerably less costly than emergency accommodation or transitional congregate facilities for families, while also offering substantial additional benefits across a range of psychosocial domains, particularly for the children (O'Sullivan, 2017; Daly, 2019).

Rather, the prevailing mantra was that 'Hubs are better than hotels', a binary that is not disputed, but it has excluded other possible options. As noted in Chapter Three, while 3,000 households with child dependants exited emergency accommodation to tenancies in Dublin between 2016 and 2018, sufficient information is not available on these exits, families' length of time in emergency accommodation and whether it was in a Family Hub, a hotel or other congregate facility, to determine if Family Hubs provide enhanced progression rates into tenancies over other forms of emergency accommodation, as has been suggested. That they are on balance better than hotels or B&B-type accommodation is a threadbare justification for a major plank of the policy response to families experiencing homelessness that requires considerable financial capital and revenue expenditure. That slightly more than half of adults experiencing homelessness were in private emergency accommodation in mid–2019, despite the addition of a new set of congregate facilities for families, is a striking feature of current responses to homelessness and the limitations of current policy responses.

Shelters

In addition to the provision of congregate transitional facilities for families from 2016 onwards, there was also a substantial increase in the number of congregate emergency and transitional facilities for singles. Nationally, there were approximately 1,900 such beds available in mid-2016, with the majority of beds in Dublin and for single men. As a result of the addition of the Family Hubs and the opening of a significant number of new shelter beds for singles, there were over 3,200 statutorily funded beds in the system by June 2019, with an expected expenditure of over €62 million in 2019 compared to just over €19 million in 2013.

Just over 100 shelters were in operation in 2019, with over half of them in Dublin. All the providers are not-for-profit bodies, and more than half of the shelters are provided by five NGOs, with one NGO alone responsible for the provision of 26 shelters across the country. The opening of further shelter beds, in addition to Family Hubs, is expected to continue in 2020. To date, little information is available on the quality of shelter services or their efficacy in progressing residents to secure accommodation. Rather, shelters are primarily about containing the problem, and the evidence noted in Chapter Three on the increasing numbers in these facilities for more than six months indicates the failure of shelters to resolve their homelessness. In Dublin, there were just 670 adults in shelters for more than six months in early 2016 but that had increased to 1,500 by the middle of 2019.

Given the well-documented limitations of congregate shelters as a response to households experiencing homelessness, their cost (both ongoing revenue and initial capital) and the difficulties in closing them down (Culhane, 1992) once opened, the construction of this massive shelter infrastructure across the country is increasingly becoming part of the problem, rather than part of the solution to ending homelessness over the next decade.

Housing First

In September 2018, a *National Housing First Implementation Plan 2018–2020* (Government of Ireland, 2018), covering the period 2018 to 2021, was launched following the reasonably successful operation of a Housing First scheme in Dublin. The plan targets rough sleepers and those in emergency accommodation on a long-term basis with high support needs, with 737 such adults identified nationally and 543 (74 per cent) in the Dublin region. Despite identifying 737 adults who met the criteria for Housing First services, the plan only proposes to create 663 tenancies, or 90 per cent of identified need, over the lifetime of the plan – approximately 220 tenancies a year – and only to create 273 tenancies in the Dublin region, exactly half the number of units relative to the number of adults identified as homeless on a long-term basis with a high support need.

The identification of 737 adults who met the criteria of sleeping rough or in emergency accommodation on a long-term basis with high support needs was collected at a point in time in December 2017. Based on current trends of just over 3,000 new presentations to homelessness services in the first six months of 2019, the number of adults in emergency accommodation for more than six months is increasing each quarter, and with the Dublin Region Homeless Executive's (2019b: 13) *Action Framework* for the period 2019–21 stating baldly that 'it is evident that the scale of homelessness will continue to grow' over the next three years, it seems clear that there will be a flow number of adults who will meet the criteria for Housing First services during the period of the plan. Thus, while the number of tenancies to be created seems ambitious based on a point-in-time analysis of need, it is less so when seen over the lifetime of the plan. Indeed, based on current trends, even if the target of 663 tenancies is achieved, it is likely that the number of adults in emergency accommodation for more than six months and/or sleeping rough will not have decreased at the end of the period in question.

Broader debates have highlighted the distinction between Housing First as a *specific programme for specific people*, and Housing First as a *philosophy* that informs the housing system and other services for people experiencing homelessness (Allen et al, 2020). In the Irish case, Housing First is a specific ring-fenced programme for a limited number of people, albeit one that, based on the existing evidence, will provide sustainable solutions for these people. However, it will not disrupt the flow of households into homelessness during the period of the plan, and will moderate, rather than reduce, the numbers in emergency accommodation for more than six months.

Preventing homelessness

Tenancy Protection Service

A Tenancy Protection Service was established by Threshold, a not-for-profit body, initially in Dublin and later expanded to adjoining and other urban areas. It was funded by the exchequer in mid-2014 to assist households living in the private rented sector at risk of homelessness due to rent increases or the termination of tenancies by providing them with an enhanced rent supplement, advocating for the tenant to maintain the dwelling and/or obtaining an alternative tenancy.

Between June 2014 and June 2019, nearly 29,000 contacts were made with the Tenancy Protection Service in Dublin, of whom over 11,700 (40 per cent) were deemed to be at risk of homelessness. Just over half of those deemed at risk of homelessness had their tenancy protected, initially through an increase in their rent supplement but increasingly through advocating for the tenant(s). For example, in the six months from June to December 2015, over 1,600 tenancies were protected by receiving a rent uplift while only 41 tenancies received an uplift in the first six months of 2019, though in just over 600 cases, Threshold was acting as an advocate for the tenants. The cost of providing these services was just under €1.2 million in 2018, not including the cost of any rent uplifts. However, as the number of rent uplifts has declined, this is a very minor cost in the overall scheme of expenditure on services for people at risk of homelessness.

This decline was largely the consequence of the introduction of rent control or pressure zones in early 2016, which stipulated: that rent cannot be reviewed upwards more than once in any 24-month period (it had been once every 12 months); an extension of notice periods for both landlords and tenants in respect of the termination of longer-term tenancies; verification procedures where the landlord intends to sell or refurbish a property and therefore terminate the tenancy; the introduction of a 4 per cent rental growth limit in designated Rent Pressure Zones (RPZs); and the extension of standard tenancies from four to six years. Although not primarily a response to the increasing number of households experiencing homelessness, given the number of households who had entered emergency accommodation from the private rented sector, this measure might nonetheless have been expected to have some positive impact.

While these measures did moderate the rate of increase in rents, rent increases in the RPZs still exceeded 4 per cent per annum (Ahrens et al, 2019). The standardised average national rent declined from nearly €1,000 a month at the commencement of the Global Financial Crisis in 2008 to just under €750 a month in Q1 2012. Rents then stabilised until early 2014, when they then increased by 60 per cent nationally between Q1 2014 and Q2 2019 to €1,200. In Dublin, the standardised average rent per month was €960 in Q1 2012 and increased by nearly 80 per cent to just over €1,700 a month in Q2 2019. Possible reasons for this rent inflation in RPZs beyond the stipulated 4 per cent include some methodological limitations in relation to the database used to determine rent inflation – the registration data of Residential Tenancies Board (the regulator for the private rented sector and Approved Housing Bodies in Ireland), which currently capture only new rents per quarter rather than the stock of all current rents – as well as that measures to assist households exit emergency accommodation and to prevent them entering in the first instance can be up to 50 per cent above the base rate for HAP.

Homeless HAP

Under the aforementioned HAP housing benefit scheme, since early 2015, discretion is given to increase the basic payment by up to 20 per cent nationally, and by up to 50 per cent for those at risk of homelessness in Dublin. In practice, in urban areas, and especially so in Dublin, this discretionary payment is now the norm rather than the exception. In the Greater Dublin area, of the just over 11,500 HAP tenancies at the end of Q1 2019, 37 per cent were in receipt of a discretionary payment of up to 50 per cent and 20 per cent were in receipt of a discretionary payment of up to 20 per cent. For example, the basic monthly HAP rate for a couple or one adult with two children in Dublin City Council is €1,275 but if the household is deemed to be at risk of homelessness or in emergency accommodation, this payment can be increased to close to €1,900.

Homeless HAP also allows local authorities to pay deposits and advance rental payments for any household experiencing homelessness. By mid-2019, there were just over 4,700 active Homeless HAP tenancies in the Dublin region, households who were either prevented from entering homelessness by receiving this payment or who had exited emergency accommodation, which was up from 683 households in 2016 (Kilkenny, 2019: 15). However, just under 6,300 Homeless HAP tenancies were created, suggesting that a relatively high rate of tenancies were terminated for various reasons. Data are not available on the reasons for tenancy terminations specifically in Homeless HAP tenancies, only for all HAP tenancies. Of the nearly 14,500 closed HAP tenancies to date (23 per cent of all tenancies created), nearly one quarter were transfers into social housing tenancies and a further quarter were voluntary terminations. The remaining transfers were either related to compliance issues or landlords exiting the market (Kilkenny, 2019: 17). Outside of Dublin, the majority of local authorities provide Homeless HAP Place Finder services that assist households to secure private rented accommodation, in addition to providing a security deposit and one month's rent in advance, but the discretionary increase is limited to 20 per cent.

Prioritising homeless households for social housing tenancies

One option available to local authorities to reduce the number of households in emergency accommodation is to increase their rate of allocation to social housing tenancies to such households. In mid-2015, a directive was issued by the Minister for Housing to increase the number of social housing allocations for households in emergency accommodation to between 30 and 50 per cent in large urban local authorities. This was seen as encouraging households to enter emergency accommodation in order to fast-track their way to social housing tenancies by Dublin local authorities, and the directive expired in April 2016. In early 2018, Dublin City Council, the authority with the single highest number of households in emergency accommodation, decided that families in emergency accommodation would no longer receive priority for social housing tenancies. The decision not to allocate a higher number of tenancies to households in emergency accommodation was based on a view that this would encourage families both to enter emergency accommodation and to stay for longer in order to secure a social housing tenancy, rather than avail of social housing support in the form of HAP. That the number of families entering emergency accommodation for the first time has increased each month, with some seasonal variation (as discussed in Chapter Two), suggests that the driver of increased numbers of presentations are not perverse incentives in the allocation system, but a lack of security in the private rented sector.

Dublin Region Homeless Executive prevention service

Also in Dublin, the Dublin Region Homeless Executive has operated a prevention service for households in the four Dublin local authorities, whereby households who present and are accepted as homeless can be provided with an immediate social housing support via Homeless HAP and, in a very small number of cases, a social housing tenancy in order to prevent them from entering emergency accommodation. Between January 2017 and June 2019, approximately 3,700 households received this enhanced support and, as a result, did not enter emergency accommodation.

Public and private expenditure on services for people experiencing homelessness

All of the services noted earlier are reactions to homelessness that are costly, both to individuals experiencing homelessness and to the public purse. Revenue or current expenditure by central (Department of Housing) and local governments on accommodation services for households experiencing homelessness nationally increased by 250 per cent from just €71.5 million in 2014 to €251 million in 2019. This figure does not include the capital funding associated with the provision of additional shelters and Family Hubs; rather, it is simply the day-to-day expenditure on providing the main emergency accommodation for households experiencing homelessness. As noted earlier in the chapter, this expenditure is distributed between not-for-profit bodies (47.5 per cent), for-profit accommodation services (45.5 per cent) and local authorities (7 per cent). Additional funding is provided by various statutory health and social inclusion services for households experiencing homelessness or for preventing homelessness (via the RS scheme funded by the Department of Employment Affairs and Social Protection in the amount of €39 million), which was estimated to be €85 million in 2017 (Homelessness Inter-Agency Group, 2018: 11).

The not-for-profit providers of services for those experiencing homelessness also generate income through various fund-raising activities, and based on the accounts of the leading ten providers, somewhere in the region of €50 million will be donated by the public to these non-for-profit bodies in 2019. Based on an expenditure of just over €45 million in the first half of 2019, total expenditure on the Homeless HAP programme, which both prevents households entering emergency accommodation in the first place and aids them in exiting shelters (see earlier), will come close to €100 million for the full year. This will exceed the total expenditure on Homeless HAP between 2016 and 2018 (Kilkenny, 2019: 10).

Excluding the revenue raised from fund-raising by NGO service providers, approximately €250 million of statutory revenue funding will be expended in 2019 on *maintaining*, on average, less than 6,000 households at any point in time in temporary and emergency accommodation services. There was a further expenditure of €150 million on *preventing* households entering emergency accommodation, or to successfully *exit* via enhanced rent allowances for the private rented housing sector. This €400 million is, in the main, ring-fenced funding for either preventing households who are assessed as at risk of homelessness or for maintaining households experiencing homelessness in temporary and emergency accommodation in 2019.

There is a further *capital expenditure* of nearly €940 million for the provision of just under 8,000 local authority and AHB housing units to be provided in 2019 (up from 4,000 units in 2016), as well as revenue funding for the general HAP and RS of over €400 million (excluding the ring-fenced funding for homeless households). While this expenditure is not ring-fenced simply for those experiencing homelessness, the provision of new social housing is crucial in assisting households to exit emergency accommodation, and in the first half of 2019, just over 670 households exited emergency accommodation to either a local authority or AHB social housing tenancy. Thus, in addition to the dedicated stream of statutory funding for homelessness services of €400 million, additional statutory capital funding for social housing to meet general housing need is also ensuring that significant numbers of households exit or do not enter emergency accommodation.

The provision of funding of social housing tenancies and supports for households at risk of homelessness or in emergency accommodation is considerable but generally seen as a good use of public funding as it provides households with secure and stable housing, though, as noted earlier, the degree of secure occupancy is considerably stronger in social housing tenancies than via supports. However, there is much unease about the costs associated with the provision of emergency accommodation, particularly with the use of private providers, as well as the steady increase in the number of shelter beds provided by various NGOs. In Dublin, where the bulk of the new shelter and Family Hub beds were provided, the revenue cost of providing supported temporary accommodation in 2019 is estimated to be nearly €64 million, up from nearly €15 million in 2014, with the spend on private emergency accommodation estimated to be in excess of €71 million in 2019, up from nearly €14 million in 2014.

Weekly expenditure on hotels and B&Bs has increased from just under €200,000 in Dublin and €11,000 outside Dublin in the first half of 2013, to over €1.5 million and nearly

€0.5 million, respectively, in the second half of 2019.[1] It was estimated by the Department of Housing that the full-year cost of keeping a family in a hotel in Dublin was just over €67,000 in 2017 (Kilkenny, 2019: 21).

In Dublin alone, nearly €135 million will be expended on emergency and temporary accommodation in 2019, or nearly 85 per cent of all budgeted expenditure on designated services for people experiencing homelessness. In addition, between 2018 and 2020, over €51 million in capital costs will be expended in Dublin alone on the provision of new congregate accommodation or refurbishing existing stock. In 2019, the four Dublin local authorities will expend €1 for every €10 euro of their entire revenue budget on designated services for people experiencing homelessness, up from €3.5 for every €100 in 2014.

Expenditure on private emergency accommodation outside of Dublin has grown rapidly, with an expenditure of just over €0.5 million in 2014 but expected to be over €23 million in 2019. In the four other major urban centres outside of Dublin (Cork, Galway, Limerick and Waterford), expenditure on services for people experiencing homelessness more than doubled from 2 per cent of all revenue expenditure in 2013 to 4.4 per cent in 2019.

In brief, in 2019, at least €250 million will be expended on providing households with temporary and emergency accommodation, the bulk of this expenditure from central and local governments, supplemented by up to €50 million through the fund-raising activities of a myriad of NGOs, with a further €150 million on targeted enhanced rent supplements to prevent households from entering emergency accommodation. In addition, increased funding for general social housing has resulted in a higher output of units, and this has assisted a significant number of households to exit emergency accommodation. Ironically, given this level of expenditure, as noted in Chapter One, in a recent HOME-EU survey, nearly 80 per cent of

Irish people surveyed believed that government spending on homelessness was too little.

The expenditure outlined earlier is on *preventing* homelessness occurring in the first instance, *providing* those who experience homelessness with emergency shelter and support, and *progressing* those in emergency accommodation to tenancies. There is an additional cost to the exchequer of not resolving homelessness: the increased use of emergency health-care services and heightened risk of negative interaction with the criminal justice system particularly of those households who experience chronic and episodic homelessness. Based on the expenditure for 2019, over the next five years, *at a minimum*, there will be ring-fenced exchequer and local government funding (excluding social services expenditure) for those households in emergency accommodation of €1.25 billion and €750 million on preventative services, with the leading NGO providers fund-raising a further €250 million.

Conclusion

A feature of the recent Irish experience is not only the massively expanded and costly infrastructure of temporary and emergency accommodation for households experiencing homelessness, but also the substantial preventative services to enable households to maintain their tenancies in the private rented sector through enhanced rent supplement payments and advocating on behalf of tenants to maintain tenancies. Support for these services has resulted in a significant increase in both revenue and capital exchequer funding.

Despite the relative success of the various schemes in protecting nearly 5,000 private rented sector tenancies, preventing a further 3,000 households from entering emergency accommodation in Dublin alone by providing them with enhanced payments to remain in or access the private rented sector, and assisting over 4,000 households to exit emergency accommodation and secure private rented tenancies at a relatively modest cost, as we saw in Chapter Three, the number of households in emergency accommodation nonetheless increased by 150 per cent between 2014 and 2019. One of the explanations for this is that in protecting tenancies in the private rented sector, the goalposts have moved. It is not so much the inability to pay increased rents that is resulting in tenancies being terminated, but the properties being withdrawn from the market, either through repossession, family use or sale.

For example, between Q3 2012 and Q2 2019, just under 5,500 buy-to-let (BTL) residential properties were repossessed with vacant possession on foot of a Court Order or voluntarily surrendered or abandoned. With over 12,300 BTL properties in arrears for over 720 days in Q2 2019 (Central Bank of Ireland, various years), repossessions of these dwellings will continue. That the number of registered private rented dwellings with the Residential Tenancies Board declined by nearly 3 per cent from 319,311 dwellings to 310,788 between Q2 2017 and Q2 2019, when demand for private rented dwellings is high and rents are increasing, suggests that in addition to repossessions by banks, landlords are validly terminating tenancies in order to use the dwellings for their own or their family's use, or to sell the dwelling.

Utilising the stock of the private rented sector to meet social housing need is critical in preventing and responding to homelessness given the sluggishness of output from local authority of AHB providers. One quarter of those residing in this sector are receiving some form of state income support to allow them to maintain their tenancy. Despite enhanced payment schemes to prevent households entering emergency services, as well as enhanced payments and supports to assist households to exit emergency accommodation, the number of households entering emergency accommodation continues to increase and the number of households exiting continues to decrease.

As noted in Chapter One, while the Housing Act 1988 did not place a specific duty on local authorities to provide accommodation for those experiencing homelessness, in practice, 'public expectations, government policy and the weight of international convention have combined to put an obligation on local authorities to act and provide assistance for homeless persons' (Lewis, 2019: 112–13). This may seem unsatisfactory in comparison with the greater rights in legislation found, for example, in the UK; indeed, advocacy groups were looking for more legislation on the rights of people experiencing homelessness in their campaign in the 1980s. However, in practice, as Lewis notes, those who present to local authorities as homeless are provided with temporary emergency accommodation pending their provision of a social housing tenancy or support. Also, as noted earlier, while not legislated for in the Housing Act 1988, as is the case in the UK, in practice, local authorities provide supports to assist households to maintain or source alternative accommodation if they face having to enter emergency accommodation, for example, due to being served with a valid notice of termination in the private rented sector. Unlike the legislation in the UK, what the Irish legislation does not include is an intentionality test. Recent legislative changes in the UK have also strengthened the role of prevention but this has raised concerns about 'the risk of unlawful gatekeeping' (Crisis, 2018: 385).

Despite the evidence presented in this chapter of the very considerable expenditure on services for people experiencing homelessness, the deployment of a plethora of plans, pillars and the majority of conventional policy tools, including a form of rent control, has failed to adequately respond to homelessness. Therefore, the Irish experience demonstrates the need to rethink how we respond to homelessness as the current response is failing. Chapter Five explores how rethinking homelessness requires a fundamental reframing of homelessness and the debunking of a range of myths that have distorted our responses to date.

Note

1 Further increases in costs are likely in 2019 for such accommodation as due to space constraints in DPCs, the Department of Justice, via the Reception and Integration Agency that has responsibility for providing accommodation for those seeking international protection, are increasingly using hotels and B&Bs at an estimated cost of €22 million in 2019 (IGEES, 2019: 25).

FIVE

Rethinking homelessness

Introduction

Based on the descriptive analysis of homelessness in the preceding chapters, this final chapter outlines why we need to rethink both our understanding of the 'causes of homelessness' and the appropriate policy responses that flow from this rethinking. If we think that people experience homelessness because of the 'quality of accommodation available' in congregate shelters and hubs, or because 'of years of bad behaviour, or behaviour that isn't the behaviour of you and me', or because people are 'gaming the system' to unfairly obtain social housing, then responses to those experiencing homelessness will take a particular path.[1] There is nothing new in this portrayal of people experiencing homelessness, nor is it unique to Ireland. For example, in his historical analysis of homeless men in the US, Kim Hopper (2003: 46) notes that such portrayals are an 'old dodge', that is:

> that the deepest truth about such men is that they fundamentally are different (if not unalterably so) from the rest of us. Such a canard has its motivating utilities, and expediency is one of them. So long as the appearance

of unusual numbers of homeless men can be framed as a temporary aberration, the fiction can be entertained that homelessness signifies nothing other than the deranged mentalities, bad habits, or faulty coping skills of those it affects.

There are somewhat more benign, but nonetheless inaccurate, claims that hold true for only a minority of those experiencing homelessness contained in the National Housing First Strategy (Government of Ireland, 2018: 9):

> [t]he multiple causes and facets of health problems mean people who are homeless have much shorter lives compared to the rest of the population, with an average life expectancy of 42 years of age (44 in males and 37 in females), compared with 82 years of age in the general population.

This may have the effect of confirming the perception that homelessness is the preserve of a damaged and deviant group of different people.

We need to rethink homelessness and plan a future where temporary housing, including both shelter and transitional housing, is replaced with locally based prevention services for those at risk of experiencing homelessness and rapid rehousing for those who do experience it. Rethinking homelessness will require substantial shifts and transformations in *policy* (from managing homelessness to ending homelessness), *practice* (to evidenced-based interventions) and *perception* (that those experiencing homelessness are not the diseased, disabled detritus of society unable or unwilling to be helped) by all actors (central government, local government and not-for-profit service providers).

We have increasing research evidence both on what works in preventing homelessness in the first instance, and on the support mechanisms that can ensure sustainable and stable accommodation for people who have experienced homelessness. This research demonstrates that policymakers need to rethink their response to homelessness as it is becoming progressively clear that while existing policies are preventing some households from entering homelessness, and assisting others to successfully exit emergency accommodation, they are not doing at sufficient scale to prevent the ongoing increase in the number of households in emergency accommodation for increasingly longer periods of time. However, in the majority of countries, responses to homelessness by both the government and NGOs remain stubbornly embedded in assumptions that homelessness is the consequence of individual-level failures or dysfunctions. As a consequence, the majority of services for people experiencing homelessness remain at the level of the provision of congregate emergency accommodation (largely for singles) or commercial hotels for families, albeit with some exceptions, such as in Finland.

Understanding homelessness as a relatively predictable event in the life cycle of those who experience entrenched housing instability and labour market precariousness, rather than the outcome of individual pathologies and inadequacies that strike, more or less randomly, at the population at large, has profound consequences for responding to homelessness. This interaction of housing and labour markets, both historically and contemporaneously, has led to the ebb and flow of households into and out of homelessness at different historical junctures. Measures such as mass social housing provision, the decommodification of health, educational and other social services, and labour market activation, for example, have reduced the flow of precarious households into homelessness, while the commodification and scaling back of such services have increased the flow into homelessness.

Recognising the drivers of homelessness as residential instability and economic precariousness would encourage policymakers to devise responses that make housing with supports available to those who will otherwise continue to traverse temporary but extraordinarily expensive responses to this instability. Our knowledge of the costs of maintaining people in homelessness via the provision of congregate emergency and temporary accommodation, as shown in Chapter Four, demonstrates that it is both fiscally responsible and ethically justifiable to provide evidence-based housing responses to people experiencing long-term homelessness, with supports where necessary (Parsell, 2017).

Housing and homelessness

The idea that housing is the key solution to preventing and ending homelessness seems self-evident. However as documented in Chapter Two, until relatively recently, the primary response by state and non-state bodies in the majority of countries was not the provision of housing, but rather the provision of congregate shelters of various shapes and sizes. This was based on the idea that those who entered shelters were inadequate, deviant or damaged, and shelter services would provide the bedrock upon which such individuals could be rehabilitated and returned to society; those incapable of rehabilitation or unwilling to be rehabilitated would be provided with a subsistence existence. The limits of shelter-based services were evident from the emergence of such services, as articulated earlier in the book. However, it was not until the end of the 20th century that rapid rehousing for those experiencing homelessness emerged in countries as diverse as the US and Finland as either a specific programme for those experiencing multiple exclusion homelessness (Padgett et al, 2016) or, somewhat uniquely in Finland, a transformation of the entire system of responding to homelessness through housing and the closure of the bulk of their shelter services (Y Foundation, 2017).

Providing housing for all is clearly the most crucial element in ending homelessness in that homelessness is, above all else, a form of residential instability brought about by the inability to secure access to, and maintain, affordable and adequate accommodation. The inability to secure and maintain accommodation varies over time and space. This is because it reflects structural factors such as housing markets, social protection systems, health policies and so on, which are variable across the Global North, in constant flux and interact with individual-level vulnerabilities. Individuals are vulnerable to homelessness when, for example, housing markets do not deliver affordable housing, social protection systems do not provide sufficient income support to counteract market rents or health systems do not provide adequate care for individuals with disabilities.

As described earlier and set out in Chapter Three, although the provision of emergency accommodation for those experiencing homelessness, usually in the form of congregate shelter facilities, is expensive, it does provide an alternative to literal homelessness, and the majority of shelter users will eventually exit the shelters. However, *rapid rehousing* into secure tenancies, with support if required, resolves individual homelessness more immediately, and initial research suggested that it was also more cost-effective. More balanced judgements now suggest that it not necessarily less costly or more effective in promoting, for example, quality of life and social integration (Latimer et al, 2019); however, if the provision of one's own accommodation with support is no more costly than the provision of congregate shelter accommodation, then it would appear sensible public policy to provide the former rather than the latter.

Both Dennis Culhane and Dan O'Flaherty, leading commentators on homelessness in the US, have further argued that some of the cost–benefit analyses can sometimes forget the bigger picture: that the objective is to provide services that work for households experiencing homelessness, not to reduce costs. As O'Flaherty (2019: 3) notes, such analyses can 'leave out the most important benefits of these programs – those that accrue to the participants and their families'. Furthermore, Culhane (2008: 109) cautions that:

the services utilization cost of homelessness is only one dimension of the moral issues raised by the problem. Other moral dimensions of homelessness include dehumanization, diminished capacity to actualize basic societal rights and privileges, and susceptibility to victimization, including violence. While less easily 'monetized' these moral dimensions reflect 'costs' to the individuals affected, as well as to society.

The key issue is that congregate shelter services are both costly and ineffective, whereas the provision of housing with support, certainly for those experiencing chronic homelessness, is effective and cost offsets may arise. As Parsell et al (2017: 1549) argue: '[a]lthough we believe that cost offsets ought not to be the primary motivator for ending chronic homelessness, the evidence about cost offsets does indeed strengthen and give additional credibility to moral arguments for supportive housing'.

Barriers to rapid rehousing

Given the success of specific Housing First programmes to effectively house those experiencing complex or multiple exclusion homelessness (Kertesz and Johnson, 2017), as well as the experience of Finland in effectively achieving functional zero in relation to those in emergency accommodation and sleeping rough through the deployment of a rapid rehousing philosophy for all those experiencing homelessness, why have other jurisdictions not employed these tactics at scale (Allen et al, 2020). Research has suggested that it is the result of the insufficient supply of social housing relative to overall demand, not simply for households experiencing homelessness, and a lack of both supply and affordability particularly in the private rented sector.

Other barriers include an entrenched attachment to a model of provision that sees the people experiencing homelessness as not ready for housing until they acquire the skills required to sustain a tenancy. For example, research commissioned for the recently published ambitious and research-evidenced 'Ending homelessness together' Scottish action plan argues that:

> The rapid rehousing approach requires a significant culture change to remove the subjective language of 'tenancy readiness' from homelessness responses altogether. The starting position is that all people, even those with the most complex needs, have the competencies required to sustain a tenancy, with the right support (Indigohouse, 2018: 58; for further details, see Anderson, 2019).

In a sophisticated analysis of all those barriers in an Australian context, Clarke et al (2019) make the crucial observation that the perceptions of service providers may be influenced more by wider housing policy, in particular, policies in relation to the allocation of scarce social housing, than by any intrinsic opposition to the philosophy of rapid rehousing. If broader housing allocations policy requires the satisfaction of various conditions to demonstrate ability to maintain a tenancy, this will result in a layer of temporary accommodation services where households are held in abeyance either until they can demonstrate compliance with these conditions or they simply wait until suitable housing becomes available.

As a consequence, declarations of the adoption of a rapid rehousing approach often simply entail a commitment to funding a specific Housing First programme for a designated group of usually multiply excluded individuals experiencing prolonged homelessness sitting uneasily alongside a broader housing allocations policy that maintains a housing-ready approach. In relation to Australia, Clarke et al (2019: 19) persuasively argue that:

> the funding of discrete Housing First initiatives is not sufficient in and of itself to improve outcomes for people

with complex needs who are experiencing homelessness. Rather, it is imperative that governments also reconfigure housing policy to ensure that Housing First providers are able to access permanent housing for their clients in a timely manner and without having to demonstrate that those clients are housing ready.

Ending homelessness will require the provision of housing: however, the provision of housing alone will not end all forms of homelessness, particularly entrenched homelessness, without providing the necessary support to maintain that housing. However, the question remains as to what type of housing is required.

The importance of social housing

Based on the robust Journeys Home data in Australia, Prentice and Scutella (2019) find that social housing has a statistically significant positive impact on reducing the likelihood of becoming homeless compared to similarly vulnerable households not in social housing due to subsidised rents, longer leases and tenancy supports. Rent supplements for those in the private rented sector are important, but in terms of protecting households, the outcomes are more modest in comparison with those residing in social housing, without providing similar levels of affordability and security of tenure. Equally, O'Donnell (2019: 21), also using Journeys Home data, concludes that '[p]eople who enter social housing are more likely to maintain their tenancy and less likely to experience homelessness or other forms of disadvantage than people living in privately rented housing'.

Three recent books have explored the future of social housing in Ireland. Eoin Ó Broin (2019: 16), a current member of the Irish parliamentary lower house and Sinn Fein spokesperson on housing, argues for a 'completely new conception of public housing from what has dominated to-date', where local authorities would provide housing for those households who are not in a position to rent or purchase at market prices. Such provision would include not only traditional subsidised tenancies, but also cost–rental properties and units for affordable purchase. Thus, the provision of social housing tenancies would move from the current position of having a residual and highly rationed 'ambulance' role, to one where non–market-based housing is provided mainly by local authorities, would meet the housing needs of 'a much broader mixture of households' and 'if delivered at sufficient scale would also provide eligible households with real alternatives to the private market thus promoting a genuinely tenure neutral system' (Ó Broin, 2019: 163). Ó Broin also argues that a legal right to a home should be enshrined in the Irish Constitution if approved by the people in a referendum – and based on the existing opinion polls, there is strong support for such a constitutional change. Such a change would not, as Ó Broin (2019: 158) acknowledges, 'mean that the following day all citizens are entitled to a house provided by the State', but rather bring about 'an important cultural shift from thinking of housing as a commodity and towards an understanding of housing as, in the first and primary instance, a home, a social good rather than as a financial asset' (Ó Broin, 2019: 159).

Norris and Hayden (2018) argue that the mixed economy of provision via local authorities, AHBs and various rent supplements works reasonably well in rural areas, but less so in urban areas, where 'housing subsidy recipients in particular had great difficulty in securing private rented accommodation'(2018: 91). Local Authority social housing is funded via capital grants from central government, resulting in reductions in output during recessionary periods and increases in expansionary periods, with associated higher costs. In addition, rents are not linked to costs, resulting in often poor maintenance of their stock and an incentive to sell council housing to tenants at a substantial loss. Ultimately, they conclude that the ability of local authorities to deliver housing supply at the scale required to meet need will require a fundamental and radical reform of the financial model underpinning delivery.

Eddie Lewis (2019), a former senior official at the Department of Housing, is equally convinced of the need to reform our social housing system. He suggests a number of pathways for the future, including: a return to the traditional model of provision of exchequer-funded social housing that would provide a safety net for low-income households; a pathway that would develop a cost-rental model for both low- and intermediate-income households, using current expenditure via HAP, with the main providers being AHBs; and a model centred around life-cycle choice that would use both capital and revenue funding, and would end the concept of a lifetime tenancy. His analysis is that current policy fits closest with the traditional model, which, in his view, is 'a high risk and high cost solution that could quickly become unsustainable' (Lewis, 2019: 309). Despite the 'rising demand for affordable rental housing and the continuation of homelessness', Lewis (2019: 321) is more pessimistic about the possibility of addressing these challenges, noting that the 'political system in Ireland is not comfortable with challenging major problems head on', preferring instead '[i]ncremental change' and 'tinkering with regulations'.

Lewis also notes the significance of the long-term government policy of facilitating the purchase of local authority houses by sitting tenants at a discounted rate in reducing the stock of housing available for letting. The tenant purchase scheme was abolished in Scotland in 2016, but Lewis is not optimistic that the policy will change in Ireland; thus, even if new-built social housing output increases over the next number of years, stock will continue to be lost via the purchase scheme.

Social housing supports via private rented housing, with tenancies supported by the HAP, will remain crucial in providing households with secure tenancies into the future, as well as for those currently exiting emergency accommodation. However, the role of private rented sector housing as a driver of homelessness as a consequence of the valid, and in some cases invalid, termination of tenancies will continue to produce a flow of households into emergency accommodation as long as landlords retain the right to validly terminate tenancies for a host of reasons other than breaches of the tenancy agreement, including family use and sale. Two arguments are generally put forward to explain why landlords must have this power: the first is that if you remove this power, landlords will not invest in the private sector, and thus rather than improving the lot of tenants, it will actually worsen their lot; and the second is specific to Ireland, where it is argued that the Irish constitution privileges the right to private property.

The first argument is a perfect example of what Albert O. Hirschman (1991: 7) called the 'perversity thesis' – that 'any purposive action to improve some feature of political, social, or economic order only serves to exacerbate the condition one wishes to remedy' – which is a standard counter-argument to progressive policies utilised for over 200 years. The same argument that landlords would flee from the market was used in 2004 when a modest degree of regulation was legislated for in respect of the private rented sector. In practice, the number of private tenancies registered with the regulatory body, the Residential Tenancies Board, increased from 85,000 in 2005 to over 310,000 by the end of 2018. On the second issue, under article 43 of the Constitution, the right to private property is not an absolute right, but rather one that is to be 'regulated by the principles of social justice', and '[t]he State, accordingly, may as occasion requires delimit by law the exercise of the said rights with a view to reconciling their exercise with the exigencies of the common good'. Thus, it can be argued that demands for constitutional change, or even the insertion of a right to housing in the Constitution, are not necessary as it is a matter of the interpretation of the Constitution that, on the face of it, principles of social justice and the exigencies of the common good would apply in preventing households from experiencing homelessness.

The direction that social housing takes will be crucial in ending homelessness, and the more pessimistic conclusion by Lewis, no doubt based on his first-hand experience, is of concern. In addition to these commentaries on the need for social housing, Lyons has estimated that, taking into account predicted population increases, net migration, urbanisation, obsolescence and household size, real demand for housing will require between 40,000 and 50,000 new dwellings per annum over the next 20 years. In addition to scale, he points out that what we build is equally important. Due to changes in household composition, we will see an increasing number of one- to two-person households, whose housing requirements will be urban apartments, which Lyons estimates will require 'an annual output of over 25,000 partments each year for the next six decades' (Lyons, 2018: 128). However, it is expected that only just over 21,000 units of housing will be completed by the end of 2019, and although a substantial increase on the low of 4,600 new units of housing completed in 2013, will nonetheless result in ongoing 'imbalances in Ireland's residential property market' (Conefrey and Staunton, 2019: 3), unmet demand, particularly in Dublin and housing costs rising faster than incomes (Kennedy and Meyers, 2019).

Conclusion

As I was completing this book in early November 2019, three events came to my attention that only confirmed my view of the importance of challenging the dominant perceptions of homelessness and the policy responses that we adopt. First, I received an email from the NGO DePaul International announcing its involvement in the World's Big Sleep Out on the night of 7 December, stating that:

> [t]he event will bring together an estimated 50,000 people in locations across the globe to sleep out under the stars in unison to create the world's largest display of

solidarity and support for those experiencing homelessness and displacement. Together, the events are aiming to raise $50 million to make a transformational impact on the lives of 1 million homeless and displaced people worldwide.

Half the expected income raised (€500,000) was intended to go to DePaul Ireland, with the balance going 'towards supporting people displaced internationally'. To my surprise, the Big Sleep Out in Dublin was to take place in the cobbled front square of Trinity College, and 2,000 people were expected to don a sleeping bag for the night and be entertained by 'on-stage performances'.

As documented in Chapter Two, 'sleep outs' convey messages that equate homelessness with rough sleeping and as best resolved through generously donating to well-intentioned NGOs, messages that are not supported by research evidence. Furthermore, as described in Chapter Four, on the basis that the statutory authorities in Ireland will spend €400 million in 2019 on preventing homelessness, providing emergency accommodation and progressing households out of homelessness, the notion that €50 million will be transformational for 1 million people experiencing homelessness across 52 cities seems fanciful at best, and disingenuous at worst.

Given that in Q2 2019, local authorities in Ireland spent €240,000 a day on maintaining households in emergency accommodation, the €500,000 that the event was expected to raise is equivalent to the cost of just over two days' accommodation. Yet, as we saw in Chapter Two, a majority of people, not only in Ireland, but across Europe, believe that the state is putting insufficient funding into services for those experiencing homelessness, and the enthusiastic, if naive, response by members of the public to fund-raising events such as sleep outs confirms this perception. The paradox whereby state funding for services for people experiencing homelessness has tripled over the past five years and yet the public perceive services to be underfunded, with a range of fund-raising efforts being required in order to ensure that services are provided, must surely be a tribute to the efforts and talents of the fund-raisers of the various not-for-profit providers.

Second, I received notice of a new documentary film on homelessness in Ireland directed by Scott Altman, entitled *Home*, which promised to shed 'light on the homeless epidemic in Dublin'. The publicity material also promised to highlight the 'often inevitable relationships between homelessness, drugs and alcohol'. Perhaps the documentary will provide a more subtle portrait of pathways to homelessness than suggested by the promotional material but the tone of the blurb suggests that the documentary will simply confirm an inaccurate perception that the reason why people experience homelessness is through their 'bad behaviour' and 'bad choices'.

Both initiatives emblemise the increasing concern that individuals have for their fellow citizens who are experiencing homelessness, the desire to expose the tragedy of homelessness and the desire to raise funds to alleviate their plight. However, both approaches are fundamentally flawed through being based on an understanding of homelessness as something experienced by defective and/or unfortunate individuals, and best resolved through individual acts of compassion through donating to underfunded NGOs in order to allow for the provision of tea and toiletries.

Third, the draft revenue budgets for 2020 for the four Dublin local authorities were published. The Dublin authorities estimate that they will spend just over €200 million on services for people experiencing homelessness in 2020, compared to just under €50 million in 2014, with the bulk of this expenditure going on emergency accommodation. This revenue expenditure will account for nearly 12 per cent of all the revenue expenditure of the four authorities, compared to 3.5 per cent in 2014. Part of the reason for the increase is that the Dublin Region Homeless Executive announced in November 2019 the opening of the largest emergency shelter for single adults in the country. Located in Dublin City centre, the shelter was to have a capacity for 155 adults. Following protests by local residents that there were already too many shelter beds for single men in that part of Dublin, the plan was quickly shelved and a 30 unit family hub will be opened instead. Galway City, where this book started, estimated that it will need a budget of €10.7 million for services for those experiencing homelessness in 2020, up from €1.8 million in 2014, or from 2.3 per cent of all revenue expenditure to 10.7 per cent.

Ending homelessness is possible but it will not be achieved through charity, compassion or caring, or through sleep outs, shelters or soup. It will require, as Johnson (2019: 53) noted in relation to Australia, a disruption of 'our existing fetish with pathological policies and our refusal to reform our housing system.' Homelessness can be ended through the large-scale provision of state-funded social housing tenancies provided by both local authorities and AHBs, with sustainable streams of funding and eliminating the current disincentives to maintaining and retaining the stock. It will also require the restoration of social housing to a 'wider affordability role', rather than 'a safety net' or 'ambulance role'. As noted in Chapter Four, the provision of social housing has increased in recent years but need substantially outstrips supply, and the ongoing policy of tenant purchase continues to denude the stock available for letting. Social housing supports for those wishing to reside in the private rented sector are also critical. However, landlord and tenant law needs to be rebalanced in order to ensure that tenancies are for as long as tenants need them, and the ability of landlords to terminate tenancies for reasons other than the non-payment of rent or damage to the property or adjacent properties is curtailed. These are the basic bedrock measures required to stop the flow of households into emergency accommodation and to provide secure tenancies into the future. If these changes do not happen, we will continue to maintain an increasing numbers of households in emergency accommodation, which as highlighted earlier is extraordinarily detrimental to the well-being of those households and costly to the exchequer. These are essentially the political and distributive issues that should shape the future direction of social housing and the ending of homelessness.

Note

[1]   These comments were made in the period 2017 to 2019 by, respectively: the Chief Executive of Dublin City Council, the local authority with the largest number of households in emergency accommodation in the country; the Director of the Dublin Region Homeless Executive, the body charged with responding to homelessness in the Dublin region; and at the time of his remarks, the Chair of the Housing Agency, a body that works 'towards delivering sustainable and affordable housing for all'.

References

Ahrens, A., Martinez-Cillero, M. and O'Toole, C. (2019) *Trends in Rental Price Inflation and the Introduction of Rent Pressure Zones in Ireland*, Dublin: Economic and Social Research Institute and Residential Tenancies Board.

Allen, M., Benjaminsen, L., O'Sullivan, E. and Pleace, N. (2020) *Ending Homelessness? The Contrasting Experiences of Denmark, Finland and Ireland*, Bristol: Policy Press.

Althammer, B. (2014) 'Transnational expert discourse on vagrancy around 1900', in B. Althammer, A. Gestrich and J. Grundler (eds) *The Welfare State and the 'Deviant Poor' in Europe, 1870–1933*, Basingstoke: Palgrave Macmillan, pp 103–125.

Althammer, B. (2016) Controlling vagrancy: Germany, England and France, 1880–1914, in B. Althammer, L. Raphael and T. Stazic-Wendt (eds) *Rescuing the Vulnerable: Poverty, Welfare and Social Ties in Modern Europe*, New York, NY: Berghahn Books, pp 187–211.

Althammer, B. (2018) 'Roaming men, sedentary women? The gendering of vagrancy offenses in nineteenth-century Europe', *Journal of Social History*, 51(4): 736–59.

Andersen, I. (2019) 'Delivering the right to housing? Why Scotland still needs an Ending Homelessness Action Plan', *European Journal of Homelessness*, 13(2): 131–159.

Aubry, T., Farrell, S., Hwang, S.W. and Calhoun, M. (2013) 'Identifying the patterns of emergency shelter stays of single individuals in Canadian cities of different sizes', *Housing Studies*, 28(6): 910–27.

Bahr, H.M. and Caplow, T. (1973) *Old Men Drunk and Sober*, New York, NY: New York University Press.

Baptista, I. and Marlier, E. (2019) *Fighting Homelessness and Housing Exclusion in Europe: A Study of National Policies*, Brussels: European Commission.

Baptista, I., Benjaminsen, L., Busch-Geertsema, V. and Pleace, N. (2017) *Family Homelessness in Europe*, Brussels: FEANTSA.

Baumohl, J. and Huebner, R.B. (1991) 'Alcohol and other drug problems among the homeless: research, practice, and future directions', *Housing Policy Debate*, 2(3): 837–66.

Benjaminsen, L. (2016) 'Homelessness in a Scandinavian welfare state: the risk of shelter use in the Danish adult population', *Urban Studies*, 53(10): 2041–63.

Benjaminsen, L. and Andrade, S.B. (2015) 'Testing a typology of homelessness across welfare regimes: shelter use in Denmark and the USA', *Housing Studies*, 30(6): 858–76.

Bibby, R.W. and Mauss, A.L. (1974) 'Skidders and their servants: variable goals and functions of the skid road rescue mission', *Journal for the Scientific Study of Religion* 13(4): 421–436.

Bloom, A. (2005) 'Towards a history of homelessness', *Journal of Urban History*, 31(6): 907–17.

Blower, E., Donald, K. and Upadhyay, S. (2012) 'The human rights implications of contemporary patterns of social control', *Journal of Human Rights Practice*, 4(2): 197–212.

Bramley, G. and Fitzpatrick, S. (2018) 'Homelessness in the UK: who is most at risk?', *Housing Studies*, 33(1): 96–116.

Bretherton, J. (2017) 'Reconsidering gender in homelessness', *European Journal of Homelessness*, 11(1): 1–21.

Busch-Geertsema, V. (2010) 'Defining and measuring homelessness', in E. O'Sullivan, V. Busch-Geertsema, D. Quilgars and N. Pleace (eds) *Homelessness Research in Europe*, Brussels: FEANTSA.

Busch-Geertsema, V. and Sahlin, I. (2007) 'The role of hostels and temporary accommodation', *European Journal of Homelessness*, 1: 67–93.

Busch-Geertsema, V., Benjaminsen, L., Filipovič Hrast, M. and Pleace, N. (2014) *Extent and Profile of Homelessness in European Member States*, Brussels: European Observatory on Homelessness.

Central Bank of Ireland (various years) *Residential Mortgage Arrears and Repossession Statistics*, Dublin: Central Bank of Ireland.

Clarke, A., Parsell, C. and Vorsina, M. (2019) 'The role of housing policy in perpetuating conditional forms of homelessness support in the era of Housing First: evidence from Australia', *Housing Studies*. doi.org/10.1080/02673037.2019.1642452

Colburn, G. (2017) 'Seasonal variation in family homeless shelter usage', *Housing Policy Debate*, 27(1): 80–97.

Conefrey, T. and Staunton, D. (2019) 'Population change and housing demand in Ireland', *Central Bank of Ireland Economic Letter,* 14: 1–16.

Corrigan, E. and Watson, D. (2018) *Social Housing in the Irish Housing Market*, Working Paper No. 594, Dublin: Economic and Social Research Institute and Department of Housing Planning and Local Government.

Crisis (2018) *Everybody In: How to End Homelessness in Great Britain*, London: Crisis.

Crowley, N. and Mullen, R. (2019) 'Framing the right to housing: a values-led approach', *European Journal of Homelessness* 13(2): 31–44.

Culhane, D.P. (1992) 'The quandaries of shelter reform: an appraisal of efforts to "manage" homelessness', *Social Service Review*, 63(3): 428–40.

Culhane, D.P. (2008) 'The cost of homelessness: a perspective from the United States', *European Journal of Homelessness*, 2(1): 97–114.

Culhane, D.P. and Kuhn, R. (1998) 'Patterns and determinants of public shelter utilization among homeless adults in New York City and Philadelphia', *Journal of Policy Analysis and Management*, 17(1): 23–43.

Culhane, D.P., Metraux, S., Byrne, T., Steno, M. and Bainbridge, J. (2013) 'The age structure of contemporary homelessness: evidence and implications for public policy', *Analyses of Social Issues and Public Policy*, 13(1): 228–44.

Daly, A., Craig, S. and O'Sullivan, E. (2018) 'The institutional circuit: single homelessness in Ireland', *European Journal of Homelessness*, 12(2): 79–94.

Daly, A., Craig, S. and O'Sullivan, E. (2019) 'A profile of psychiatric in-patient admissions with no fixed abode (NFA) 2007–2016', *Irish Medical Journal*, 112(1).

Daly, M. (2019) *National Strategies to Fight Homelessness and Housing Exclusion – Ireland*, Brussels: European Social Policy Network and European Commission.

Department of the Environment, Community and Local Government (2013) *Homelessness Policy Statement*, Dublin: Department of the Environment, Community and Local Government.

Department of Housing, Planning, Community and Local Government (2016) *Rebuilding Ireland: Action Plan for Housing and Homelessness*, Dublin: Department of the Environment, Community and Local Government.

DeVerteuil, D., May, J. and Von Mah, J. (2009) 'Complexity not collapse: recasting the geographies of homelessness in a "punitive" age', *Progress in Human Geography*, 33(5): 646–66.

Doherty, V. (1982) *Closing Down the County Homes*, Dublin: Simon Community (National Office).

Dublin Region Homeless Executive (2019a) *Reported Reasons for Family Homelessness in the Dublin Region July to December 2018*, Dublin: Dublin Region Homeless Executive.

Dublin Region Homeless Executive (2019b) *The Homeless Action Framework for Dublin, 2019–2021*, Dublin: Dublin Region Homeless Executive.

Edgar, B. and Doherty, J. (eds) (2001) *Women and Homelessness in Europe*, Bristol: Policy Press.

Expert Group (2019) *Traveller Accommodation: Expert Review*, Dublin: Department of Housing, Planning and Local Government.

Fahey, T. and Watson, D. (1995) *An Analysis of Social Housing Need*, Dublin: Economic and Social Research Institute.

Farrell, N. (1988) *Homelessness in Galway*, Galway: Focus on Shelter Coalition.

Fazel, S., Geddes, J.R. and Kushel, M. (2014) 'The health of homeless people in high-income countries: descriptive epidemiology, health consequences, and clinical and policy recommendations', *The Lancet*, 384: 1529–40.

Fazel, S., Khosla, V., Doll, H. and Geddes, J. (2008) 'The prevalence of mental disorders among the homeless in Western countries: systematic review and meta-regression analysis', *PLoS Med*, 5(12): e225.

Fitzgerald, E. (1990) 'Housing at a turning point', in J. Blackwell, B. Harvey, M. Higgins and J. Walsh (eds) *Housing: Moving into Crisis*, Dublin: National Campaign for the Homeless and Combat Poverty Agency, pp 9–17.

Fitzpatrick, S. (1998) 'Homelessness in the European Union', in M. Kleinman, W. Matznetter and M. Stephens (eds) *European Integration and Housing Policy*, London: Routledge, pp 197–214.

Fitzpatrick, S. and Pawson, H. (2016) 'Fifty years since Cathy Come Home: critical reflections on the UK homelessness safety net', *International Journal of Housing Policy*, 16(4): 543–55.

Gerstal, N., Bogard, C.J., McConnell, J.J. and Schwartz, M. (1996) 'The therapeutic incarceration of homeless families', *Social Services Review*, 70(4): 543–72.

Goluboff, R. (2016) *Vagrant Nation: Police Power, Constitutional Change, and the Making of the 1960s*, New York, NY: Oxford University Press.

Government of Ireland (2018) *National Housing First Implementation Plan 2018–2020*, Dublin: Government of Ireland.

Gowan, T. (2010) *Hobos, Hustlers and Backsliders: Homeless in San Francisco*, Minneapolis: University of Minnesota Press.

Greenwood, R.M. (2015) *Evaluation of Dublin Housing First Demonstration Project: Summary of Findings*, Dublin: Dublin Region Homeless Executive.

Grotti, R., Russell, H., Fahey, É. and Maître, B. (2018) *Discrimination and Inequality in Housing in Ireland*, Dublin: Irish Human Rights and Equality Commission and Economic and Social Research Institute.

Hanna, E. (2013) *Modern Dublin: Urban Change and the Irish Past, 1957–1973*, Oxford: Oxford University Press.

Hart, M.G. (1927) 'Farm colonies for misdemeanants (a bibliography)', *Journal of Criminal Law and Criminology* 17(4): 626–39.

Harvey, B. (1985) 'Administrative responses to the homeless', *Administration*, 33(1): 131–40.

Harvey, B. (2008) 'Homelessness, the 1988 Housing Act, state policy and civil society', in D. Downey (ed) *Perspectives on Irish Homelessness: Past, Present and Future*, Dublin: Homeless Agency, pp 10–14.

Hayden, A. (2014) 'Local authority rented housing: the path to decline, 1966–1988', in L. Sirr (ed) *Renting in Ireland: The Social, Voluntary and Private Sectors*, Dublin: Institute of Public Administration, pp 107–120.

Hearne, R. and Murphy, M. (2018) 'An absence of rights: homeless families and social housing marketisation in Ireland', *Administration*, 66(2): 9–31.

Henwood, B.F., Wenzel, S.L., Mangano, P.F., Hombs, M., Padgett, D.K., Byrne, T., Rice, E., Butts, D. and Uretsky, M.C. (2015) *The Grand Challenge of Ending Homelessness*, Working Paper No. 9, Cleveland, OH: American Academy of Social Work and Social Welfare.

Hirschman, A.O. (1991) *The Rhetoric of Reaction: Perversity, Futility, Jeopardy*, Harvard, MA: Belknap Press.

Homeless Agency (2006) *Counted in 2005*, Dublin: Homeless Agency.

Homelessness Inter-Agency Group (2018) *Report to the Minister for Housing, Planning and Local Government*, Dublin: Homelessness Inter-Agency Group.

Hopper, K. (1989) 'Deviance and dwelling space: notes on the resettlement of homeless persons with drug and alcohol problems', *Contemporary Drug Problems*, 16: 391–414.

Hopper, K. (1990) 'Public shelter as "a hybrid institution": homeless men in historical perspective', *Journal of Social Issues*, 46(4): 13–29.

Hopper, K. (1997) 'Homelessness old and new: the matter of definition', in D.P. Culhane and S.P. Hornburg (eds) *Understanding Homelessness: New Policy and Research Perspectives*, Washington, DC: Fannie Mae Foundation, pp 9–67.

Hopper, K. (2003) *Reckoning with Homelessness*, Ithaca, NY: Cornell University Press.

Hopper, K. and Baumohl, J. (1994) 'Held in abeyance: rethinking homelessness and advocacy', *The American Behavioral Scientist* 37(4): 522–52.

Hopper, K., Jost, J., Hay, T., Welber, S. and Haugland, G. (1997) 'Homelessness, severe mental illness, and the institutional circuit', *Psychiatric Services*, 48(5): 659–64.

IGEES (Irish Government Economic and Evaluation Service) (2019) *Direct Provision: Overview of Current Accommodation Expenditure*, Dublin: Department of Justice and Equality.

Indigohouse (2018) *Scotland's Transition to Rapid Rehousing: Market Area Analysis, Legislative and Culture Review*, Glasgow: Scottish Government's Homelessness and Rough Sleeping Action Group.

Johnsen, S. and Fitzpatrick, S. (2010) 'Revanchist sanitisation or coercive care? The use of enforcement to combat begging, street drinking and rough sleeping in England', *Urban Studies*, 47(8): 1703–23.

Johnsen, S., Fitzpatrick, S. and Watts, B. (2018) 'Homelessness and social control: a typology', *Housing Studies*, 33(7): 1106–26.

Johnson, G. (2019) 'Australia – getting out of the policy quagmire', in Lassy, J. and Turunen, S. (eds) *Homelessness in 20230: Essays on Possible Futures*, Helsinki: Y- Foundation, pp 50–53.

Johnson, G., Scutella, R., Tseng, Y.P. and Wood, G. (2019) 'How do housing and labour markets affect individual homelessness?', *Housing Studies*, 34(7): 1089–116.

Joint Committee on Housing, Planning and Local Government (2018) *Examination of Local Authority Housing Lists*, Dublin: Houses of the Oireachtas.

Kärkkäinen, S.L. (1996) *Homelessness in Finland*, Helsinki: Stakes.

Kelleher, C., Kelleher, P. and McCarthy, P. (1992) *Patterns of Hostel Use in Dublin*, Dublin: Focus Point.

Kennedy, G. and Myers, S. (2019) 'An overview of the Irish housing market', *Central Bank of Ireland Financial Stability Notes* 16: 1–21.

Kennedy, S. (1985) *But Where Can I Go? Homeless Women in Dublin*, Dublin: Arlen House.

Kertesz, S. and Johnson, G. (2017) 'Housing First: lessons from the United States and challenges for Australia', *Australian Economic Review*, 50(2): 220–8.

Kilkenny, P. (2019) *Housing Assistance Payment, 2014–2019*, Dublin: Department of Public Expenditure and Reform.

Kuhn, R. and Culhane, D.P. (1998) 'Applying cluster analysis to test a typology of homelessness: results from the analysis of administrative data', *American Journal of Community Psychology*, 17(1): 23–43.

Latimer, E.A., Rabouin, D., Cao, Z., Ly, A., Powell, G., Adair, C.E., Sareen, J., Somers, J.M., Stergiopoulos, V., Pinto, A.D., Moodie, E.E. and Veldhuizen, S.R. (2019) 'Cost-effectiveness of Housing First intervention with intensive case management compared with treatment as usual for homeless adults with mental illness: secondary analysis of a randomized clinical trial', *JAMA Network Open*, 2(8): e199782.

Lawless, M. and Corr, C. (2005) *Drug Use Among the Homeless Population in Ireland: A Report for the National Advisory Committee on Drugs*, Dublin: Stationery Office.

Leonard, F. (1966) '"Helping" the unemployed in the nineteenth century: the case of the American tramp', *Social Service Review* 40(4): 429–34.

Lewis, E. (2019) *Social Housing Policy in Ireland: New Directions*, Dublin: Institute of Public Administration.

Long, A.E., Sheridan, S., Gambi, L. and Hoey, D. (2019) *Family Homelessness in Dublin: Causes, Housing Histories and Finding a Home*, Dublin: Focus Ireland.

Lyons, R. (2018) 'Ireland in 2040: urbanization, demographics and housing', *Journal of the Statistical and Social Inquiry Society of Ireland*, XLVII: 122–8.

McCarthy, P. (1988) *A Study of the Work Skills, Experience and Preferences of Simon Community Residents*, Dublin: Simon Community (National Office).

McCarthy, P. and Conlon, E. (1988) *A National Survey of Young People Out-of-Home in Ireland*, Dublin: Streetwise National Coalition.

Mackie, P., Johnsen, S. and Wood, J. (2019) 'Ending street homelessness: what works and why we don't do it', *European Journal of Homelessness*, 13(10): 85–96.

Maeseele, T., Roose, R., Bouverne-De Bie, M. and Roets, G. (2014) 'From vagrancy to homelessness: the value of a welfare approach to homelessness', *British Journal of Social Work*, 44(7): 1717–34.

Maher, I. (1989) 'Grafting the homeless on to the housing code', *The Irish Jurist (NS)*, 24(2): 182–197.

Maphosa, P. (2018) *Census 2016: Homeless Results*, Dublin: Dublin Region Homeless Agency.

Mayock, P. and Bretherton, J. (2016) *Women's Homelessness in Europe*, London: Palgrave Macmillan.

Mayock, P., Sheridan, S. and Parker, S. (2015) *The Dynamics of Long-Term Homelessness Among Women in Ireland*, Dublin: Dublin Region Homeless Executive.

Ministry of Health (1930) *Report of the Departmental Committee on the Relief of the Casual Poor*, London: Stationery Office.

Mitchell, D. (2001) 'Postmodern geographical praxis: postmodern impulses and the war against homeless people in the "Post Justice City"', in: C. Minca (ed) *Postmodern Geography: Theory and Practice*, Oxford: Blackwell, pp.57–92.

Mitchell, D. (2018) 'From Boise to Budapest: capital circulation, compound capitalist destruction and the persistence of homelessness', in A. Albet and N. Benach (eds) *Gentrification as a Global Strategy: Neil Smith and Beyond*, London: Routledge, pp 99–111.

Montgomery, A.E., Metraux, S. and Culhane, D.P. (2013) 'Rethinking homelessness prevention among persons with serious mental illness', *Social Issues and Policy Review*, 7(1): 58–82.

Moore, J. (1994) *B&B in Focus: The Use of Bed and Breakfast Accommodation for Homeless Adults in Dublin*, Dublin: Focus Point.

Morrin, H. (2019) *Family Progression through Homeless Services: 2016–2018*, Dublin: Dublin Region Homeless Executive.

Ní Cheallaigh, C., Cullivan, S., Sears, J., Lawlee, A.M., Browne, J., Kieran, J., Segurado, R., O'Carroll, A., O'Reilly, F., Creagh, D., Bergin, C., Kenny, R.A. and Byrne , D. (2017) 'Usage of unscheduled hospital care by homeless individuals in Dublin, Ireland: a cross-sectional study', *BMJ Open*. 2017 Dec 1;7(11):e016420. doi: 10.1136/bmjopen-2017-016420

Norris, M. and Byrne, M. (2017) 'A tale of two busts (and a boom): Irish social housing before and after the global financial crisis', *Critical Housing Analysis*, 4(2): 19–28.

Norris, M. and Fahey, T. (2014) 'Conclusions', in M. Norris (ed) *Social Housing, Disadvantage and Neighbourhood Liveability: Ten Years of Change in Social Housing Neighbourhoods*, London: Routledge, pp 219–28.

Norris, M. and Hayden, A. (2018) *The Future of Council Housing: An Analysis of the Financial Sustainability of Local Authority Provided Social Housing*, Dublin: The Community Foundation for Ireland.

Nowicki, M., Brickell, K. and Harris, E. (2019) 'The hotelisation of the housing crisis: experiences of family homelessness in Dublin hotels', *The Geographical Journal*, 183(3): 313–24.

O'Brien, J. (1981) 'Poverty and homelessness', in S. Kennedy (ed) *One Million Poor? The Challenge of Irish Inequality*, Dublin: Turoe Press, pp 76–92.

O'Brien, L. and Dillon, B. (1982) *Private Rented: The Forgotten Sector*, Dublin: Threshold.

Ó Broin, E. (2019) *Home: Why Public Housing is the Answer*, Dublin, Merrion Press.

O'Donnell, J. (2019) 'Does social housing reduce homelessness? A multistate analysis of housing and homelessness pathways', *Housing Studies*, DOI: 10.1080/02673037.2018.1549318

O'Donoghue-Hynes, B., Waldron, R. and Redmond, D. (2018) 'Using administrative data from a national shared services database to target the delivery of homeless services in the Dublin region', paper presented at the International Conference for Administrative Data Research, Queen's University, Belfast, 21 June.

O'Flaherty, B. (2004) 'Wrong person and wrong place: for homelessness, the conjunction is what matters', *Journal of Housing Economics*, 13: 1–15.

O'Flaherty, B. (2019) 'Homelessness research: a guide for economists (and friends)', *Journal of Housing Economics*, 44: 1–25.

O'Flynn, A. (2016) *Time for Change: A Research Study on Begging in Dublin City Centre*, Dublin: Dublin City Council.

O'Kennedy, P. (2016) *The Lost Boys of Galway*, Galway: Shantalla Press.

O'Sullivan, E. (1993) 'Identity and survival in a hostile environment: homeless men in Galway', in C. Curtin, H. Donnan and T.M. Wilson (eds) *Irish Urban Cultures*, Belfast: Institute of Irish Studies, pp.161–80.

O'Sullivan, E. (1995) 'Section 5 of the Child Care Act 1991 and youth homelessness', in H. Ferguson and P. Kenny (eds) *On Behalf of the Child: Child Welfare, Child Protection and the Child Care Act 1991*, Dublin: A & A Farmar, pp 84–104.

O'Sullivan, E. (2008) 'Sustainable solutions to homelessness: the Irish case', *European Journal of Homelessness*, 2: 203–231.

O'Sullivan, E. (2016a) 'Women's homelessness: a historical perspective', in P. Mayock and J. Bretherton (eds) *Women's Homelessness in Europe*, London: Palgrave Macmillan, pp 15–40.

O'Sullivan, E. (2016b) 'Ending homelessness in Ireland: ambition, austerity, adjustment', *European Journal of Homelessness*, 10(1): 11–40.

O'Sullivan, E. (2017) 'International commentary: family options study – observations from the periphery of Europe', *Cityscape: A Journal of Policy Development and Research*, 19(3): 207–13.

O'Sullivan, E. and Mayock, P. (2008) 'Youth homelessness in Ireland: the emergence of a social problem', *Youth Studies Ireland*, 3(1): 15–29.

O'Sullivan, E. and O'Donnell, I. (2007) 'Coercive confinement in Ireland: the waning of a culture of control', *Punishment and Society: The International Journal of Penology*, 9(1): 27–44.

O'Sullivan, E. and O'Donnell, I. (eds) (2012) *Patients, Prisoners and Penitents: Coercive Confinement in Ireland*, Manchester: Manchester University Press.

Padgett, D., Henwood, B.F. and Tsemberis, S.J. (2016) *Housing First: Ending Homelessness, Transforming Systems, and Changing Lives*, New York: NY, Oxford University Press.

Parsell, C. (2017) 'Do we have the knowledge to address homelessness?', *Social Service Review*, 91(1): 134–53.

Parsell, C. (2018) *The Homeless Person in Contemporary Society: Identities, Agency, and Choice*, Abingdon: Routledge.

Parsell, C. (2019) 'Growing wealth, increasing homelessness, and more opportunities to exercise our care to the homeless', *European Journal of Homelessness*, 13(2): 13–26.

Parsell, C. and Watts, B. (2017) 'Charity and justice: a reflection on new forms of homeless provision in Australia', *European Journal of Homelessness*, 11(2): 65–76.

Parsell, C., Petersen, M. and Culhane, D. (2017) 'Cost offsets of supportive housing: evidence for social work', *British Journal of Social Work*, 47(5): 1534–53.

Parsell, C., Clarke, A. and Vorsina, M. (2019) 'Evidence for an integrated healthcare and psychosocial multidisciplinary model to address rough sleeping', *Health and Social Care in the Community*, DOI: 10.1111/hsc.12835

Petit, J., Loubiere, S., Tinland, A., Vargas-Moniz, M., Spinnewijn, F., Manning, R., Santinello, M., Wolf, J., Bokszczanin, A., Bernad, R., Kallmen, H., Ornelas, J. and Auquier, P. (2019) 'European public perceptions of homelessness: a knowledge, attitudes and practices survey', *PLoS ONE*, 14(9): e0221896, https://doi.org/10.1371/journal.pone.0221896

Phelan, J.C. and Link, B.G. (1999) 'Who are "the homeless": reconsidering the stability and composition of the homeless population', *American Journal of Public Health*, 89(9): 1334–8.

Pleace, N. (2016) 'Excluded by definition: the under-representation of women in European homelessness statistics', in P. Mayock and J. Bretherton (eds) *Women's Homelessness in Europe*, London: Palgrave Macmillan.

REFERENCES

Pleace, N., Baptista, I. and Knutagård, M. (2019) *Housing First in Europe: An Overview of Implementation, Strategy and Fidelity*, Brussels and Helsinki: Housing First Europe Hub.

Pleace, N., Baptista, I., Benjaminsen, L. and Busch-Geertsema, V. (2013) *The Costs of Homelessness in Europe*, Brussels: European Observatory on Homelessness.

Prentice, D. and Scutella, R. (2019) 'What are the impacts of living in social housing? New evidence from Australia', *Housing Studies*, DOI: 10.1080/02673037.2019.1621995.

Reeve, K. (2018) 'Women and homelessness: putting gender back on the agenda', *People, Place and Policy*, 11(3): 165–74.

Rooney, J.F. (1980) 'Organizational success through program failure: skid row rescue missions', *Social Forces*, 58(3): 904–24.

Scanlon, K. and Whitehead, C., with Edge, A. and Udagawa, C. (2019) *The Cost of Homeless Services in London*, London: London School of Economics and London Councils.

Snow, D.A., Anderson, L. and Koegel, P. (1994) 'Distorting tendencies in research on the homeless', *American Behavioral Scientist*, 37(4): 461–75.

Snow, D.A., Baker, S.G., Anderson, L. and Martin, M. (1986) 'The myth of pervasive mental illness among the homeless', *Social Problems*, 33(5): 407–23.

Stark, L.R. (1987) 'A century of alcohol and homelessness: demographics and stereotypes', *Alcohol, Health and Research World*, 11: 8–13.

Stephens, M. and Fitzpatrick, S. (2007) 'Welfare regimes, housing systems and homelessness: How are they linked?', *European Journal of Homelessness*, 1(1): 201–12.

Taylor, S. and Johnson, G. (2019) *Service Use Patterns at a High-Volume Homelessness Service: A Longitudinal Analysis of Six Years of Administrative Data*, Melbourne: Unison Housing Research Lab.

Tsai, J., Lee, C.Y.S., Shen, J., Southwick, S.M. and Pietrzak, R.H. (2019) 'Public exposure and attitudes about homelessness', *Journal of Community Psychology*, 47(1): 76–92.

Tsemberis, S. (2010) 'Housing First: ending homelessness, promoting recovery and reducing costs', in I.E. Gould and B. O'Flaherty (eds) *How to House the Homeless*, New York, NY: Russell Sage Foundation, pp 37–56.

Waldron, R., O'Donoghue-Hynes, B. and Redmond, S. (2019) 'Emergency homeless shelter use in the Dublin region 2012–2016: utilizing a cluster analysis of administrative data', *Cities*, 94: 143–52.

Walsh, D. (2015) 'Psychiatric deinstitutionalisation in Ireland 1960–2013', *Irish Journal of Psychological Medicine*, 32(4): 347–52.

Watts, B., Fitzpatrick, S. and Johnsen, S. (2018) 'Controlling homeless people? Power, interventionism and legitimacy', *Journal of Social Policy*, 47(2): 235–52.

Wooden, M., Bevitt, A., Chigavazira, A., Greer, N., Johnson, G., Killackey, E., Moschion, J., Scutella, R., Tseng, Y., and Watson, N. (2012) 'Introducing Journeys Home', *Australian Economic Review*, 45(3): 368–78.

Wusinich, C., Bond, L., Nathanson, A. and Padgett, D.K. (2019) ' "If you're gonna help me, help me": barriers to housing among unsheltered homeless adults', *Evaluation and Program Planning*, 76 101673. doi: 10.1016/j.evalprogplan.2019.101673

Y Foundation (2017) *A Home of Your Own: Housing First and Ending Homelessness in Finland*, Helsinki: Y Foundation.

Index